Oracle Solaris 11: First Look

A sneak peek at all the important new features and functionality of Oracle Solaris 11

Philip P. Brown

PUBLISHING

BIRMINGHAM - MUMBAI

Oracle Solaris 11: First Look

First published: January 2013

Production Reference: 1210113

Published by Packt Publishing Ltd.
Livery Place
35 Livery Street
Birmingham B3 2PB, UK.

ISBN 978-1-84968-830-7

www.packtpub.com

Cover Image by Sandeep Vaity (sandeep.vaity@yahoo.com)

Credits

Author
Philip P. Brown

Reviewers
Alan Pae

Brian Craft

Acquisition Editor
Rukhsana Khambatta

Commissioning Editor
Meeta Rajani

Technical Editors
Hardik Soni

Ankita Meshram

Copy Editors
Alfida Paiva

Aditya Nair

Brandt D'Mello

Laxmi Subramanian

Ruta Waghmare

Project Coordinator
Michelle Quadros

Proofreaders
Maria Gould

Stephen Swaney

Lindsey Thomas

Indexer
Monica Ajmera Mehta

Graphics
Aditi Gajjar

Production Coordinators
Aparna Bhagat

Prachali Bhiwandkar

Melwyn D'sa

Nitesh Thakur

Cover Work
Prachali Bhiwandkar

About the Author

Philip P. Brown was introduced to computers at the early age of 10, by a Science teacher at St. Edmund's College, Ware, UK. He was awestruck by the phenomenal power of the ZX81's 3 MHz, Z80 CPU, and 1 K of RAM, showcasing the glory of 64 x 48 monochrome block graphics! The impressionable lad promptly went out and spent his life savings to acquire one of his very own, and then spent many hours keying in small BASIC programs such as "Ark Royal", a game where you land a block pretending to be an aircraft, on a bunch of lower blocks pretending to be an aircraft carrier. Heady stuff!

When birthday money allowed expanding the ZX81 to an unbelievable 16 K of RAM, he also felt the need to acquire a patch cable to allow him to actually save programs to audio cassettes. Once this was deployed to the family cassette recorder, he was not seen or heard from for many months that followed.

Phil's first exposure to Sun Microsystems was at U.C. Berkeley in 1989, as part of standard computer science classwork. Students were expected to do their classwork on diskless Sun 3/50 workstations running SunOS 4.1.1. During this time, he wrote his first serious freeware program, "kdrill", which at one time was part of the official X11 distribution, and remains in some Linux distros to this day. He eventually acquired a Sun workstation for personal use (with a disk and quarter-inch tape drive) and continued his home explorations, eventually transitioning from SunOS to Solaris, around Solaris 2.5.1.

The principles of the original, pre-GPL freeware licenses prevalent in 1989 inspired Phil the most. Led by their example, he has contributed to an assortment of free software projects along the way. A little-known fact is that he is responsible for "MesaGL" morphing into the modern GLX/OpenGL implementation it is known for today. At the time, MesaGL was primarily an OpenGL workalike with a separate, non-X11 API, as author Brian Paul did not believe that it could function in a speed-effective way. In 2003, Phil wrote the first GLX integration proof-of-concept code, which convinced Brian to eventually commit to true GLX extension support.

In 2002, Phil created pkg-get, inspired by Debian's apt-get utility, and started off CSW packaging. This, at last, brought the era of network-installed packages to Solaris. All major public Solaris package repositories prior to Solaris 11 still use pkg-get format catalogs for their software.

In reality, Phil also had an impact on the existence of Solaris itself. In 2002, Sun Microsystems was on the road to canceling Solaris x86 as a product line. The community was outraged, and a vote in the old "solarisonintel" Yahoo! group resulted in six community representatives making the case for x86 to Sun. Phil was one of those six who eventually flew to Sun HQ to meet the head honchos and banish the forces of evil for a while.

Phil's current hobbies include writing (both articles and code), riding motorcycles, reading historical fiction, and keeping his children amused.

The Solaris-specific part of his website is `http://www.bolthole.com/solaris`.

Most of his writing until this point has been done online, for free. His website has a particular wealth of Solaris information, and includes a mix of script writing, driver code, and Solaris sysadmin resources.

As far as books go, he was only a prepublication reviewer for *Solaris Systems Programming*, *Rich Teer*. However, the first time any of his articles got published was in *Rainbow* magazine (a publication for the Tandy Color Computer) on page 138 of the May 1989 issue, under a column named *Tools for Programming BASIC09* (`http://ia700809.us.archive.org/26/items/rainbowmagazine-1989-05/The_Rainbow_Magazine_05_1989_text.pdf`).

I would like to thank my family for being supportive and patient with me while I wrote this book. I would also like to thank many people on "the Nets", who volunteered to review a chapter for me. It was a pleasant surprise to suddenly be flooded with more volunteers than I have chapters in this book!

About the Reviewers

Alan Pae started with Novell Netware, and then being forced onto SCO Unix, his first foray into the world of Unix was not one of choice. Seeing what it could do compared to other operating systems at the time was, however, a real eye-opener. Unix could easily do things that he simply couldn't do with any other operating systems that he could run. After that, he had a chance to run Lotus Notes on some old SPARC gear as a test pilot program, and became hooked. It's been fun watching the new versions roll and the incremental improvements over the years. Solaris 10 started to break the incremental mold and make some radical changes. Solaris 11 continues in this vein, and for him, it's a much improved operating system.

I would like to thank Philip P. Brown for allowing me to make suggestions for this book, and to the staff at Packt Publishing for guiding this project to completion.

Brian Craft was introduced to Unix as a graduate student in molecular biology and biochemistry. He took a part-time detour involving SunOS, followed by Solaris 2.5.1, which quickly turned into a full-time distraction. Many years later, Brian finds himself still working with Solaris as a system administrator.

www.PacktPub.com

Support files, eBooks, discount offers and more

You might want to visit www.PacktPub.com for support files and downloads related to your book.

Did you know that Packt offers eBook versions of every book published, with PDF and ePub files available? You can upgrade to the eBook version at www.PacktPub.com and as a print book customer, you are entitled to a discount on the eBook copy. Get in touch with us at service@packtpub.com for more details.

At www.PacktPub.com, you can also read a collection of free technical articles, sign up for a range of free newsletters and receive exclusive discounts and offers on Packt books and eBooks.

http://PacktLib.PacktPub.com

Do you need instant solutions to your IT questions? PacktLib is Packt's online digital book library. Here, you can access, read and search across Packt's entire library of books.

Why Subscribe?
- Fully searchable across every book published by Packt
- Copy and paste, print and bookmark content
- On demand and accessible via web browser

Free Access for Packt account holders

If you have an account with Packt at www.PacktPub.com, you can use this to access PacktLib today and view nine entirely free books. Simply use your login credentials for immediate access.

Instant Updates on New Packt Books

Get notified! Find out when new books are published by following @PacktEnterprise on Twitter, or the *Packt Enterprise* Facebook page.

Table of Contents

Preface

Solaris 11 has had many changes in just about every area of the operating system. The difference between Solaris 10 and 11 is as great, if not greater, than the difference between Solaris 9 and 10. Filesystems, networking, zone management, and even installation of the OS itself have drastically changed. This book will help you take advantage of them to best effect.

What this book covers

Chapter 1, IPS – The Image Packaging System, details how to use the new software package system.

Chapter 2, Solaris 11 Installation Methods, gives specific examples and case studies of how to use the new OS install methods that Solaris 11 uses.

Chapter 3, Sysadmin Configuration Differences, covers the differences in day-to-day procedures that the average Solaris administrator needs to know.

Chapter 4, Networking Nuts and Bolts, delves into the fancier options and configurations now available in Solaris 11 networking.

Chapter 5, NWAM – NetWork AutoMagic, shows how to use the new auto-configuring network tool.

Chapter 6, ZFS –Now You Can't Ignore It, covers the new mandatory ZFS filesystem.

Chapter 7, Zones in Solaris 11, explores the new features and functionality of zones.

Chapter 8, Security Improvements, covers the new mandatory security auditing, as well as some other improvements.

Chapter 9, Miscellaneous, has a few things that are don't fit elsewhere.

Appendix A, IPS Package Reference; *Appendix B, New ACL Permissions and Abbreviations*; and *Appendix C, Solaris 10 Available Enhancements* – gives a few handy lists of command options.

What you need for this book

This book will be helpful to you, if you actually have a test Solaris box to play with. If you happen to have a spare SPARC (T series or M series only) or x86 machine laying around to test on, that's great. This book will show you a few different methods for installation. Otherwise, you may wish to experience Solaris 11 through a Virtual Machine (VM).

Oracle provides pre-made downloadable images for the free VirtualBox VM system. To use this, you will require at least 1 gigabytes of free RAM, and ideally more than 10 gigabytes of free disk space. Get the VM software from `http://www.virtualbox.org` and then do a web search for "solaris 11 vm download". This should take you to the current Oracle page for downloading the VM image itself.

Who this book is for

This book is intended for sysadmins who have had some experience with Solaris 10, and are either considering whether to upgrade, or just want to be aware of all major changes when they do.

Conventions

In this book, you will find a number of styles of text that distinguish between different kinds of information. Here are some examples of these styles, and an explanation of their meaning.

Code words in text are shown as follows: "To limit `pkg search` to only search package names, we must use a modifier of `pkg.fmri:`."

A block of code is set as follows:

```
<publisher name="solaris">
    <origin name="http://pkg.oracle.com/solaris/release"/>
</publisher>
```

Any command-line input or output is written as follows:

```
$ pkg info gzip|grep FMRI
```

New terms and **important words** are shown in bold. Words that you see on the screen, in menus or dialog boxes for example, appear in the text like this: "Don't choose **Automatically** for your networking type choice, unless you are installing to a laptop or workstation."

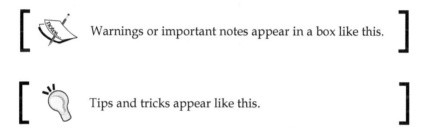

Warnings or important notes appear in a box like this.

Tips and tricks appear like this.

Reader feedback

Feedback from our readers is always welcome. Let us know what you think about this book — what you liked or may have disliked. Reader feedback is important for us to develop titles that you really get the most out of.

To send us general feedback, simply send an e-mail to feedback@packtpub.com, and mention the book title via the subject of your message.

If there is a topic that you have expertise in and you are interested in either writing or contributing to a book, see our author guide on www.packtpub.com/authors.

Customer support

Now that you are the proud owner of a Packt book, we have a number of things to help you to get the most from your purchase.

Errata

Although we have taken every care to ensure the accuracy of our content, mistakes do happen. If you find a mistake in one of our books—maybe a mistake in the text or the code—we would be grateful if you would report this to us. By doing so, you can save other readers from frustration and help us improve subsequent versions of this book. If you find any errata, please report them by visiting http://www.packtpub.com/support, selecting your book, clicking on the **errata submission form** link, and entering the details of your errata. Once your errata are verified, your submission will be accepted and the errata will be uploaded on our website, or added to any list of existing errata, under the Errata section of that title. Any existing errata can be viewed by selecting your title from http://www.packtpub.com/support.

Piracy

Piracy of copyright material on the Internet is an ongoing problem across all media. At Packt, we take the protection of our copyright and licenses very seriously. If you come across any illegal copies of our works, in any form, on the Internet, please provide us with the location address or website name immediately so that we can pursue a remedy.

Please contact us at copyright@packtpub.com with a link to the suspected pirated material.

We appreciate your help in protecting our authors, and our ability to bring you valuable content.

Questions

You can contact us at questions@packtpub.com if you are having a problem with any aspect of the book, and we will do our best to address it.

1
IPS – The Image Packaging System

This chapter introduces the new **Solaris packaging system**. The first part will introduce key concepts to be understood. The second part will give specific examples of the most common tasks a sysadmin will need to perform.

The details about installing a new Solaris machine from scratch are covered in *Chapter 2, Solaris 11 Installation Methods*, in this book. This chapter primarily deals with package management on an already running Solaris 11 system.

If you wish to try out Solaris 11 package management commands without going through the hassles of a full install, Oracle provides freely downloadable VM images of Solaris 11 – for both VirtualBox and VMWare – that are ready to go out of the box.

The brave new world of IPS

Solaris 11 has an all new packaging system for OS-related packages, in which the packages are primarily accessed via the pkg command. This new command handles the acquisition/downloading of OS packages, as well as local installation and removal of the files on local storage.

Legacy format packages, also known as **System V Release 4 (SVR4)** style packages, are still supported; pkgadd and related commands still work. This is not merely for third-party developers. Oracle itself still distributes some Solaris 11-related packages in SVR4 packages.

Even though Oracle has not stopped using SVR4 packages, the new pkg interface has some notable benefits, such as extra hooks to integrate safely with zones, and automatic use of **ZFS** snapshots for certain types of package upgrades. It is for this reason that Solaris 11 does not support **UFS** as a root filesystem. The new packaging system requires ZFS for part of its standard operations.

This chapter breaks down the concepts of the new package system into four main areas:

- An overview of package repositories
- Understanding package naming
- Understanding conceptually how packages are installed
- Practical use of the pkg command

The majority of the chapter is taken up with the practical use section.

Repositories/repos

The new pkg style is primarily network-based, rather than file-based.

While it has recently become possible to transfer a single .p5i package via the file transport mechanism of your choice, you lose the automatic upgrade capability of IPS. For that, it requires a **repository** to be running somewhere (commonly referred to as a **repo**). That said, it is certainly possible to have a copy of the full Solaris repository on your own machine.

A point of interest is that the new pkg system is differential-based in an attempt to be network efficient. If you have an older version of a package, and if you request that a new version be installed, it will only pull the newer files from the repository server, rather than the entire package.

The good news (or bad news) is that the default repo is provided by Oracle itself at oracle.com. It is a highly robust and high-bandwidth public server. Because of this, it is no longer strictly required to have a fully up-to-date local repository for network installs. You can get by with a small bootstrap image somewhere.

It is important to note that Oracle most likely logs access to its repo, so you should probably not be updating a score of machines from it unless you are confident of your licensing status.

It is possible to have a locally running repository server if you wish. Oracle provides a **Repository Image** download in the same place where it provides regular ISO image downloads for Solaris 11. If you do decide to run a repository yourself, the standard **Service Management Facility (SMF)** name for the IPS-specific service is `svc:/application/pkg/system-repository`. More details on how to do this is given in the *Creating your own IPS repository and packages* section in this chapter.

It is also possible to serve a local repository out using **NFS** and using `file:///` style URLs to access it. However, Oracle recommends using the custom server at this time.

Repository URIs, also known as origins

A Solaris machine is configured to know about a particular repository, using a repository URI. This type of URI is sometimes referred to as an **origin**.

It is actually possible to access multiple, separate repositories via the same repository URI as long as they are provided by separate **publishers**. The standard publisher name used for the Solaris OS is "solaris", not "oracle".

An IPS client is configured to point to one or more publisher-repository combinations as a source for packages.

The standard Oracle URI for Solaris 11 is `http://pkg.oracle.com/solaris/release`.

To configure your system to know about it (even though it is already known), you can use the following command:

```
pkg set-publisher -g http://pkg.oracle.com/solaris/release solaris
```

This tells your system the URI to use for the publisher named `solaris`.

It should be noted that, while the address of an IPS repository is given with an `http:` or `https:` URL, the repository itself is not browsable with a web browser in the way you might expect. While the Oracle repository server does allow a web browser to connect and even query packages, there is no single link that says "here, download the package you want". For that, you have to use the appropriate client-side tool.

Package naming schemes

Packages are now named and referred to with a naming scheme that is somewhat similar to the SMF style naming introduced in Solaris 10.

Package references in the IPS format look like this:

```
pkg:/somebase/leafname@version,num-here
pkg://publisher/somebase/leafname@version,num-here
```

Specific examples of the previously mentioned IPS format are:

```
pkg:/runtime/java/jre-6@1.6.0.0-0.175.0.0.0.2.0
pkg://solaris/runtime/java/jre-6@1.6.0.0-0.175.0.0.0.2.0
```

Note that even though both the standard Solaris repository URL and the publisher component from the previously mentioned `pkg` FMRI have the string `solaris` in them, they are in completely different namespaces. Changing one would not affect the other.

The good news in this confusion is that, as with SMF, you can use short forms most of the time. For example, the following commands all give the same output:

- `pkg list pkg://solaris/runtime/java/jre-6`
- `pkg list pkg:/runtime/java/jre-6`
- `pkg list /runtime/java/jre-6`
- `pkg list runtime/java/jre-6`
- `pkg list jre-6`

In summary, for most uses, you can ignore everything to the right of the @ symbol in the FMRI, and to the left of any forward slashes (/) in the FMRI, in order to get a short form name.

The bad news is that, sometimes, a short form that you might expect to work does not work. So, if an abbreviated form turns up nothing for a command, make sure to try the long form as well, and/or wildcards.

 For most purposes, you can ignore the version part after the @ sign, even for long form purposes. The version part only really matters at times when you have to consider whether or not to update a package.

Understanding the quirks of pkg name references

Note that, at the current moment in time, Oracle uses package naming and version information inconsistently.

First of all, the same package may have two different long forms. Taking a package at random, let's examine the installed `gzip` package. The first two listings in the following output show it as `/compress/gzip`.

However, the full information on the package, via `pkg info`, gives a longer reference for the `gzip` package (calling it an FMRI), with the additions of `/solaris` and extra numbers in the version part of it. More details on version numbers will be given later on, in the next section.

Once again, there is good news and bad news. The bad news is that these inconsistencies exist when they shouldn't. The good news is that the `pkg` system is somewhat flexible about accepting any of the variants as input most of the time. So, reading the output becomes simpler, if you can train yourself as to which parts can be safely ignored.

A comparison between the different output types is as follows:

```
$ pkg search gzip
PACKAGE
pkg:/compress/gzip@1.3.5-0.175.0.0.0.2.537

$ pkg list gzip
NAME              VERSION
compress/gzip     1.3.5-0.175.0.0.0.2.537

$ pkg info gzip|grep FMRI
FMRI
pkg://solaris/compress/gzip@1.3.5,5.11-0.175.0.0.0.2.537:20111019T091246Z
```

As mentioned previously, the `@` version parts can usually be ignored. So the thing of interest then becomes the `//solaris` component. This is an artifact of the network source of the package.

In this case, `solaris` is not the product or package name, but what Oracle chose to name the publisher of this set of packages in its repository. The full output of the `pkg list gzip` command would show this as the case.

99 percent of Solaris users will most likely be using only one publisher (`solaris`), so this component can usually be ignored.

Understanding pkg FMRI version fields

Note that the version indicator (the stuff to the right of the @ sign) must be strictly numeric at this time. This may cause problems if one tries to match some "freeware" programs up with this scheme, where letters (a, b, c, and d) are used as a part of the version number scheme as well.

As demonstrated earlier, the version part is unfortunately used inconsistently by Oracle at this time.

Some subcommands of the `pkg` command display it as @{release}-{branch}. For example:

pkg:/compress/gzip@1.3.5-0.175.0.0.0.2.537

For other subcommands, the same package may be displayed as @{release},{build}-{branch}. For example:

pkg://solaris/compress/gzip@1.3.5,5.11-0.175.0.0.0.2.537

For packages provided with Solaris itself, the {build} section (here, 5.11) is described by Oracle as being the version of the OS under which it was compiled, in this case, Solaris 11, or SunOS 5.11.

The 0.175 in Oracle Solaris packages represents a particular build number of Solaris branch that folks external to Oracle might think of as the subrelease identifier or perhaps similar to a patch level. All packages associated with that subrelease of Solaris seem to get a branch identifier mostly in the same numeric range. An earlier release of Solaris 11 seems to have mostly 0.151 as its associated branch identifier, whereas the 11/11 release seems to mostly have 0.175.0 as a branch identifier Solaris 11.1 uses 0.175.1.

Overview of package and patch installation

In this section we'll first summarize the old system of packages and patching before covering how they have changed.

The traditional methods

The old style of packages had only three basic pieces of information for a sysadmin to care about:

- The package name; for example, SUNWcsr
- The package description/name; for example, core binaries
- The package version (and corresponding patch level)

All of this information was mostly contained in the package itself. To update it, you should either have installed an entirely new version of the package, or applied a patch, which would have updated one or more packages to different patch versions.

Prior to Solaris 11, patches were downloaded and applied manually unless you used a tool such as **PCA** or Sun's **smpatch** utility. Then, even if you applied the package, there was a slight disconnect between the **package version** and the **patch level** of a package.

Previously, new Sun/Oracle packages were copied from a DVD (physical or virtual image) and then manually applied. New vendor packages were similarly copied, or sometimes downloaded, unless you had a network-aware tool such as **pkg-get**, which is similar to Debian's **apt-get**.

Now, things are very different. Almost every facet mentioned previously has changed with Solaris's new pkg system.

New Solaris 11 patch and package installation methods

With IPS, new OS patches, packages, and even new minor OS versions are all handled via a unified mechanism. If there is a bugfix available for a package, it comes in the form of a newer version of that package. There are no more hidden patch levels internal to a package; variants of a particular version of a package generate a new branch of a version. It is no longer possible to have multiple patches applied to a single package; you always have only a single version of it, with a single, unique number-based identifier for it.

Practical examples of pkg command usage

This section of the chapter contains practical examples of how to use the pkg command. This section will not describe all options and usage methods as there are many possible options. Just the most useful are shown here, in detail.

Automatic package dependency use

It is important to note that, at times, requesting that a single package be installed results in multiple packages being installed.

Installation dry run

One of the new beneficial features is the ability to do an installation dry run. You can find out basic or detailed information on what the impact to your system will be. Given that requesting a single package install may trigger a cascade of 10, 20, or more required dependencies, having a dry run is useful for those systems where disk space or bandwidth may be at a premium.

The following command will tell you how many packages will be installed, how many services will be affected, and whether a backup Boot Environment will be created as a safety measure:

```
pkg install -n [pkg-list ...]
```

To also find out how much space will be used, we can add the -v option, as follows:

```
pkg install -nv pkg-list
```

Finding packages that you want

When you are looking for a particular piece of functionality, you first need to decide whether you wish to look by package name or by filename.

One of the commands you can use is the pkg search command.

It is crucial to note, however, that the pkg search command is multifaceted. It can search for more than just filenames. Among other things, it can also search for basenames of files as well as full paths. It can also search for dependencies of packages and descriptions of packages.

Because of this, if you *only* want to search for a filename, it is best to limit its search to only be on filenames or you may get much more output than you actually need. The best way to do this is given later in this chapter.

There is a shortcut for searching package names (rather than files) called the pkg list command. By default, it only works for already-installed packages. It gives additional information regarding whether a package is installed, not installed, or frozen, if you use the -a command option.

There is unfortunately some amount of overlap between the pkg search and pkg list subcommands. There is also some slight incompatibility between valid search strings for each of them, as mentioned in the following tip.

Sysadmins familiar with **grep** — the most common sysadmin search tool — will expect that, if your search pattern matches anything in a line, that line will show up. Searches in pkg are more similar to shell-level wildcarding. However, there are some inconsistencies even with that comparison.

pkg search and pkg list have a different set of matching rules from grep, and sometimes, they are slightly different even from each other.

To limit pkg search to only search package names, we must use the following modifier: pkg.fmri.

However, even using that, we will note the following inconsistency:

- The pkg search pkg.fmri:/system/zones command fails to return a value
- The pkg list /system/zones command correctly returns the full package FMRI

Unlike the filename search, it is best *not* to use a leading / for package name searches even though the actual search results contain one. That way, both tools will match similarly, albeit with slightly different output.

- The pkg search pkg.fmri:system/zones command returns a match
- The pkg list system/zones command returns a match
- The pkg search pkg.fmri:zones command returns a match
- The pkg list zones command returns a match

Searching by filename (pkg search)

Sometimes, you are looking for a tool and want to know what package to install to get it.

If you already know the key filename you are interested in and have it conveniently in a cut-and-paste buffer, you can use the following type of command:

```
pkg search -r /full/path/to/filename
```

Otherwise, you can use wildcards if needed. The most important thing is to start the filename search with a / character.

 The pkg search command searches multiple levels of information, such as filenames, package names, descriptions, and so on. If you want to avoid voluminous output, be sure to give it some hint of what layer of information you wish to search through.

The -r flag stands for "remote" and ensures that you search the remote listing of what is actually available rather than what you have already installed.

In contrast, if you have a particular local file and want to know the package name for it, you can search with the local flag, -l.

pkg search -l some-filename

Be warned that the pkg search command thinks it is "smart" and that it knows what you want better than you do. For people who are used to using grep, this can be counterintuitive.

If for example, you are trying to find the package containing the command /usr/bin/zonestat, the following will work:

- pkg search zonestat
- pkg search /usr/bin/zonestat

Unfortunately, neither of the following will work:

- pkg search bin/zonestat
- pkg search usr/bin/zonestat

 It is important to note that even though normal pkg search output has no leading /, you are required to put one in your search string or a leading wildcard; otherwise, it will not return anything.

For filename searches, unlike other search types such as pkg name, you cannot use a multisegment match of the right-hand side. You must match the entire path exactly, or exactly the end part (the "basename" component), or else, you must use a wildcard. Wildcard styles that work are similar to the following:

- pkg search '*bin/zonestat'
- pkg search '*/zonestat'

If you wish to search for an exact match of the last component only, and if you wish to be a little more efficient than the last wildcard search shown, you can use a special indexed file search modifier, as shown in the following command:

pkg search basename:zonestat

Searching by package names (pkg search)

If you would like to avoid learning multiple ways to search for packages and don't care about knowing the installed status of a package, you can also search for package names using the `pkg search` command. However, this general search tool may pull up much more information related to a package than just its name. To avoid unnecessary output, add the modifier `pkg.fmri:` in front of your search token.

Generally speaking, `pkg search pkg.fmri:NAME` and `pkg list -a NAME` will match the same things. However, the output will be different. For one thing, `pkg list` output is usually formatted to fit in 80 columns, and so may be preferable in many cases.

Searching by package names (pkg list)

When searching for packages, a subcommand has been provided that can be easier than the general `pkg search` tool. Using `pkg list` leads to slightly cleaner output.

Remember that, as mentioned earlier, these commands do not behave like `grep` style searching.

Let's say you are looking for information about the following installed package: `pkg:/developer/build/make`.

All the following commands will work (although some may match additional packages):

- `pkg list /developer/build/make`
- `pkg list developer/build/make`
- `pkg list build/make`
- `pkg list '*/make'`
- `pkg list '*make*'`
- `pkg list make`

The following commands will *not* work to match `pkg:/developer/build/make`:

- `pkg list /build/make`
- `pkg list 'make*'`

So, as you can see, you need to match the whole line, except when you don't (ha ha). The important thing is to match whole words, and in particular, the rightmost words. Matching from the left-hand side does not work unless you use wildcards. Note that unlike filename searches, you can get away with doing multiple right side token matches with `pkg` names rather than rightmost only. That is to say that searching for `"build/make"` will match `"pkg:/developer/build/make"`. In contrast, if you were attempting to do a filename search of a similar name that way, you would not find it.

If you wish to search for those packages that are available for install on the remote server, you can add the `-a` flag to `pkg list`. If using a search that has multiple matches, you should take note of which packages may be installed already.

```
pkg list -a editor/*
```

The command will tell you which editors you have installed support for, versus which additional ones may be available to download. In the following abbreviated output for this command, the `dia` package is not installed, the `gedit` package is already installed, and the `ghex` package is flagged as being "obsolete".

NAME (PUBLISHER)	VERSION	IFO
editor/diagram/dia	0.97.1-0.175.0.0.0.0.0	---
editor/gedit	2.30.4-0.175.0.0.0.2.0	i--
editor/ghex	2.24.0-0.175.0.0.0.0.0	--o

Listing files in a package

Let's say that you are considering removing a package but are not sure what this will affect. To find out which files will be removed by a `pkg remove` operation, you can use the following command:

```
pkg contents pkg/name
```

Alternatively, if you are curious about the contents of a package that has not yet been installed, you must add the `-r` flag to query the remote side for information.

Searching for installation groups

This procedure might be more commonly associated with installation time; however, sometimes (even after initial installation), you want to upgrade an existing installation from a "bare-bones" system to a more fully-fledged set of packages.

There are a few predefined collections of packages, somewhat akin to the old `Core/Developer/Full` package cluster choices. They are organized under the `group` subdivision of Oracle's FMRI listings for Solaris 11.

The ones that are currently visible are as follows:

- `group/system/solaris-auto-install` (the default small system install)
- `group/system/solaris-desktop`
- `group/system/solaris-large-server`
- `group/system/solaris-small-server`

There are a few different ways with which you can view which groups are available from the repo server. Any of the following commands will work; they just generate output in different formats:

- `pkgrepo list -s http://pkg.oracle.com/solaris/release \`
  `'group/system/*'`
- `pkg info -r 'group/system/*' | grep Name`
- `pkg list -a 'group/system/*'`

Less-used pkg commands

There is an assortment of other day-to-day `pkg` subcommands that can be found in the manpage, some of which are avoid, unavoid, fix, revert, mediator, freeze, unfreeze, variant, and facet.

However, after 20 years of observing the problems generated by people using similar features on other systems, my recommendation to you is to avoid all of the previously mentioned advice entirely and stick to the basics. One of the worst things to have to debug as a sysadmin is attempting to repair a seemingly normal system on which you've forgotten that you did something clever a year or three back.

The one additional rarely used command I shall take time to mention is the `history` command.

pkg history [-l]

This command will give you a history of all `pkg` related activity on the machine timestamped. If you want to identify an activity at a particular time of interest, you can then use the `-l` flag to get more details.

Dealing with repositories

At the current point in time, there are not too many public IPS repositories running. That said, it is good to know how to query them. As briefly mentioned just now, the `pkgrepo` tool is the command to interact with repositories at the top level.

To find the repositories that your system is currently using, you can use the following command:

```
pkg publisher
```

You can then take the URI field from each of the output lines and run pkgrepo against it.

Official Oracle URIs for repositories are usually of the following format:

```
http://host.on.network/publisher/XXXXXXX
```

Once you have the URI of the repository you are interested in, you can query it for high-level information such as how many total packages are in the repository and the last time it was updated, as shown in the following output:

```
pkgrepo info -s http://pkg.oracle.com/solaris/release
```

This command will lead to the following output:

PUBLISHER	PACKAGES	STATUS	UPDATED
solaris	4292	online	2011-11-09T15:23:27.281209Z

Do note that, for some reason, Oracle has chosen the publisher in this case to be solaris, rather than oracle, so there is some unexpectedness in naming choices to get used to.

One advantage of using the pkgrepo command over the pkg command is that you can query packages from repos that are not currently configured as your current installation source.

```
pkgrepo list -s http://pkg.oracle.com/solaris/release \
'group/system/*'
```

While it is also possible to do a similar search with the pkg search -s http://... command, the output format of pkgrepo, in this case, is more readable, at least to me.

You can also use pkgrepo to get a list of potentially useful properties that the administrators of the repo may have set (somewhat akin to ZFS properties, using zfs get).

For example, the following command lets you know that there is a mirror of the Oracle repository available:

```
pkgrepo get -p all  -s http://pkg.oracle.com/solaris/release \
repository/mirrors
```

The preceding command will lead to the following output:

```
PUBLISHER  SECTION     PROPERTY  VALUE

solaris    repository  mirrors   (http://pkg-cdn1.oracle/com/solaris/
release/)
```

Creating your own IPS repository and packages

At some point, you may wish to create your own IPS repository, particularly if you wish to have some custom scripts applied to automated installs. The old jumpstart "finish script" concept no longer exists; instead, hooks are given to load in custom services, which must be referenced through custom packages. Or, you may simply wish to have a local copy of the Solaris packages available.

Before you can create a package, you must first create a local repository. The old workflow of generating a single `file.pkg` to distribute is gone. The new tools are geared towards uploading files directly into a repository.

Creating a local repo

Happily, creating a simple repository with no access controls is relatively easy, so long as you follow the guidelines of always doing your packaging work on the same system that your repository lives on.

To make a repo in a designated directory, such as `/var/pkgrepo`, you just need to initialize the directory with the magic tool, as follows:

```
pkgrepo create /var/pkgrepo
```

This creates the directory, and a single master file inside it, called `pkg5.repository`.

If you plan on serving many files to many machines, Oracle recommends that you create a separate `zfs` filesystem for it, with access time (`atime`) turned off, for example:

```
zfs create somepool/repo
```

```
zfs set atime=off somepool/repo
```

Once you have created the basic top-level repo, you will want to create a publisher section. This can be done for your own company or for a copy of outside repositories, or both.

Copying the Oracle Solaris repository

The publisher designation for Solaris packages is not `oracle.com` but `solaris`. Therefore, if you plan to create a local copy of Solaris packages, you will effectively be setting up a mirror for the publisher named `solaris`.

Once you have created the top-level repository, use the `pkgrecv` command to mirror all packages in the Oracle repository to it. We can use the following command:

`pkgrecv -s http://pkg.oracle.com/solaris/release -d /var/pkgrepo '*`

Once that is done, you can override the default settings for where the system gets the Solaris packages by using the following command:

`pkg set-publisher -g http://your.repo.url solaris`

Creating your own company repository

Creating a namespace for your own company is easy. You simply need to set aside a designated publisher area for it, as shown in the following command:

`pkgrepo add-publisher -s /var/pkgrepo "yourcompany.com"`

Creating a package

Unlike the SVR4 `pkg` creation tools, you should normally dedicate an entire, untouched directory tree for your package creation efforts.

For clarity, let's presume a standard location for this that we'll call `/stageroot`.

Then, when you would normally install a program to `/usr/local/bin/prog`, for packaging purposes, it will get installed to `/stageroot/usr/local/bin/prog`.

Once you have assembled all the contents of your potential package under `/stageroot`, you must then generate a manifest for it with the following command:

`pkgsend generate /stageroot >mypkg.mf`

Next, you need to give the package an identity. This can be done by adding a single line, such as the following command, anywhere in the `mypkg.mf` file to designate its identity:

`set name=pkg.fmri value=pkg://yourcompany.com/prog@1.0`

Keep in mind that the `value` field can be as simple, or as complicated, as you like, within the boundaries of the IPS package naming scheme previously mentioned. For example, you may instead choose it to be `pkg://yourcompany.com/utils/lowlevel/prog@1.0.1-75`.

Uploading packages to the repository

Now that you have a complete manifest file and a staged tree of files for your package contents, you may integrate your package into your repository. This only takes one command, as follows:

```
pkgsend publish -s /var/pkgrepo -d /stageroot mypkg.mf
```

> The pkgsend command will happily publish the exact same package collection multiple times, resulting in redundant packages in your repository. Be sure you have your versioning correct.

If the `publish` subcommand is completed successfully, you should be able to see the new version of your package, with the following command:

```
pkgrepo -s /var/pkgrepo list
```

Technically, it is quite possible to publish a package from normally installed program locations (that is to say, without a `/stageroot` prefix). Unfortunately, the IPS tools do not support the same functionality as the old `pkgproto` utility, which used to let you pass it a simple list of files and would then do the rest. This was allowed for relatively safe automated strategies such as:

```
find /usr/local -newer xyz | pkgproto >prog.template
```

Instead, with IPS, you would be required to hand-edit the manifest to have the needed paths in it, after which you could run the `publish` step without the `-d` option. However, this may lead to the creation of incomplete packages. Therefore, it is recommended that you use the method just explained, using the full but previously empty `/stageroot`.

Configuring machines to use your local repository

Once you can see your new packages successfully with a local test via `pkgrepo`, it is appropriate to open up access to the repository for other machines that need it.

The simplest way to do that is to share that directory via NFS and allow machines in your network to use your new repository. This can be done with the help of the following command:

```
pkg set-publisher -O /net/servername/var/pkgrepo yourcompany.com
```

Alternatively, you can set up a full IPS package server by configuring and enabling the `application/pkg/server` SMF service, as follows:

```
svccfg -s application/pkg/server setprop pkg/inst_root=/var/pkgrepo
svccfg -s application/pkg/server setprop pkg/readonly=true
//optionally, change the port number it runs on, with
svccfg -s application/pkg/server setprop pkg/port=(someportnum)

svcadm refresh application/pkg/server
svcadm enable application/pkg/server
```

> If you have stuck with our example location of `/var/pkgrepo`, you will not actually have to mess around with `svccfg` properties. The default `pkg/inst_root` location is `/var/pkgrepo`. The default port is 80.

If you follow the SMF route, you will be able to configure clients with the following command:

```
pkg set-publisher -O http://your.server yourcompany.com
```

Once you have set a publisher entry for your custom repository, you should be able to run normal `pkg` commands on any client machines, thus:

```
pkg install prog
```

Or, you can use:

```
pkg install pkg://yourcompany.com/prog
```

Package updates and patching

As mentioned in the first half of this chapter, patching as a separate process no longer exists. To patch, you must upgrade to a newer version of the software package in question.

At a simple level, to update all packages on your system, if newer versions are available on your configured repository, you can just run the following command:

```
pkg update
```

If you are unsure whether you need to run an update or would like to know which packages need an update first, you can use the following command:

```
pkg list -u
```

If you want to downgrade a package, or similarly, do not want to upgrade it to the latest version, you can also call the update subcommand with a specific version of a package *if* it is available, for example:

```
pkg update somepkg@1.2.3
```

That being said, Solaris packages are usually locked into a particular set of revisions via a meta package called entire. It is normally not possible to manually install a package from a newer release of Solaris 11: one must first explicitly upgrade to a newer **entire** package. To see the available versions, use the following command

```
pkgrepo list -s (repo_url) entire
```

If you have chosen to previously set up your own repository for Solaris, (as mentioned in the first part of this chapter, by downloading your own Solaris Repository Image from Oracle), you might add your own local repository. As pkg update and pkg install will by default install the latest version of a package, if it finds that multiple are available, there is not much risk involved in having this available as a fallback.

Here's an example of configuring your own repository to be the primary source for Solaris packages, with the Oracle site as a backup:

```
pkg set-publisher -g http://your.site solaris
pkg set-publisher -m http://pkg.oracle.com/solaris/release solaris
```

Gaining access to the latest versions of Solaris packages (that is, patch updates) requires a support contract to get access to a private repository. Full details for this can be found at:

```
https://pkg-register.oracle.com/
```

Summary

The new IPS package tools are a drastic change for anyone used to the long-time standard of SVR4 style packages in Solaris. Where to get them has changed. How to get them has changed. How to install and uninstall them has changed. How to list and query them has changed. Even the style of naming packages has changed.

There are some similarities to popular Linux package management tools but there are differences as well. IPS is truly a system unto itself and requires some unique learning.

While it is possible to continue using the old tried-and-true SVR4 packaging for in-house software, being a Solaris 11 system administrator requires learning at least the basics covered in the first half of this chapter. While it may not be required to know how to set up and create your own packages, it is critical that the System Administrator understands the basics of IPS package administration.

For a quick reference of IPS commands, see the *Appendix A, IPS Package Reference,* part of this book.

2

Solaris 11 Installation Methods

This chapter attempts to describe how the new Solaris 11 install system differs from the old commonplace Solaris installer system. The differences are quite significant.

It's the Oracle of install systems!

Oracle databases have the reputation of being extremely flexible, extremely scalable, and extremely difficult to configure and tune, relative to other systems.

The bad news is, Solaris 11 installation methods have gone the same way, to the point where Oracle's installation docs are now an all new 200-page PDF document (Oracle document *E21798, Installing Oracle Solaris 11 Systems*).

The good news is, this chapter will let you know about the majority of what you need to know, in a considerably smaller amount of space.

More good news:

If all you wish to do is manually install one or two systems directly from a CD image, it is still relatively simple. Things get more complicated only when you wish to do preconfigured installs. This is because jumpstart has been completely replaced, and even wanboot has been changed.

The following topics are covered in this chapter:

- Default passwords
- Installation from CD-ROM (LiveCD, Text-install, or Automated Install)
- Overview of Automated Install
- Network bootstrap process

- Install servers
- Common traps and pitfalls
- Solaris release version versus supported version

The first part of this chapter will address the simple case of installing from physical media. Each section after that, will build on knowledge from prior sections. So be sure to read this chapter from the start, to however deep you want to go, rather than just jumping into the middle somewhere.

Default passwords

Keep in mind that the normal login is `root/solaris`. There is also an auxiliary account, `jack/jack`, that is used in certain rare situations. So if the root password doesn't work at a prompt, you might want to try `jack`.

Installation from CD-ROM

Installation from physical media is almost the same as prior versions of Solaris. Simply answer some questions about filesystems, hostname, networking and so on, and you're off to the races.

However, here are a few things that you should know, even with the simple installation method:

1. There is no longer "an install image". There are now two standard flavors to choose from: **Text Install** or **Automated Installer** (**AI**). This will be explained in more detail in the later sections of this chapter, but the short answer is: If you're installing from physical media, you probably need the Text Install image.

2. No more GUI install mode. This isn't such a big deal, as GUI mode has been not much more than a slow wrapper around the text installer for a while now. However, it was occasionally nice to be able to use multiple windows and adjust font sizes, and so on.

3. There is an optional **LiveCD** (or now called **Live Media**, since it does not fit on a CD) image available, for x86 only. This is "kindasorta-butnotquite" a GUI installer. It is fairly handy for trying out Solaris x86 in a pinch, and to have the capability to install itself to disk. The drawback is, it only installs itself to disk. That's great if you want to perform a generic desktop install, but not so great if you want to install a server. It will install an exact copy of the package set on the media, without asking you any fine tuning questions. More detail on it are mentioned in the later sections.

4. Similar to the Live Media option, there is a USB media image option that is now downloadable. Once again, this is unfortunately for x86 only.

Once you deploy your chosen image, simply answer more or less the same questions you are used to answering with prior Solaris Text Install menus. This will have you on your way relatively quickly, with just a few caveats mentioned later in the *Common traps and pitfalls* section.

The x86 LiveCD install

The x86-only LiveCD has the benefit of being fully GUI-driven, and comes with features such as wireless networking ready to go, even if you install nothing to hard disk.

One drawback of doing an initial install from LiveCD, is that it installs the LiveCD OS installation to your disk, almost as-is. You get a pretty GUI that offers you almost no choices besides partitioning, language, and time zone. That being said, you can always use the `sysconfig` command after reboot to re-answer those and other questions, such as naming service and Kerberos use.

For security conscious people, you will be happy to know that it prompts you for a new user and password to use for the on-disk install, so you will not be left with the security hole of a known user and password.

 The password you set for this user will also be the initial password for root (not to mention that the user will be **sudo**-enabled). So make it a good one, or change it ASAP.

Another potential drawback is that it will install a set of packages suitable for desktop use if you don't want to waste space and management on packages that you may not need. Specifically, it will install the IPS package grouping, `group/system/solaris-desktop`. Currently, this contains over 800 packages.

If you would rather stick to a minimal set of packages, you can choose to start from one of the other ISOs available to you.

Make sure to read the *Common traps and pitfalls* section of this chapter for some other important points.

Choosing Text Install image or Automated Install image

If you don't wish to use the Live Media, or you are on SPARC, you must still choose between two different ISO images to download: The **Text Install** image or the **Automated Install** image.

I usually hate table comparisons, but making a choice between these two seems to merit one.

	Text install ISO image	AI ISO image
ISO size	450 MB	285 MB
/usr size	1.1 GB	500 MB
pkg set on disk	solaris-server-large	solaris-auto-install
Recovery disk capable	Yes	Yes
Runtime package count	464	335
Disk space required by default	5 GB	7 GB
Default install source	Local ISO	Network
Capable of both local and network installation?	Yes	Yes
Add extra packages from pkg.oracle.com?	Yes	Yes

This table hopefully will help you to decide which image to install from. If you are still unsure, you can choose the larger text installer image. It makes a better **emergency disk**, as it can do a full install even without network connectivity.

Details on installing from either of the images are given in later sections. But first, here are some more specifics on the previously mentioned set of comparisons.

When you boot into a shell from the AI image, you will have only the `group/system/solaris-auto-install` set of packages (335). In contrast, the Text Install image comes with the `group/system/solaris-large-server` set of packages (464).

Both make for a decent system recovery disk. They both have full ZFS tools and other core tools, plus a full set of kernel drivers. However, the Text Install image comes with other fancy stuff, such as nano, Java, CUPS printing, not to mention manpages. (This requires 500 MB more on an installed disk, if you let it do its normal install). It also has everything it needs in its own disk image, rather than downloading from the network, so may be faster to install. Both images require a network if you wish to install desktop related packages.

Oddly, even though the AI image is smaller, by default it requires a *larger* disk to install. Or at least the installer program insists on having one. However, there are ways around that, such as not using the AI installer program.

Manually invoking the install programs

It turns out that the AI image defaults to calling a program named `auto-install`, and the Text Installer defaults to calling a program named `text-install`. However, both are present in both disks, so you can technically use either method, with either disk.

It's good to know that while neither of the ISO images give you the entire set of Solaris packages, you can easily install the full set over the network, directly from Oracle. No special configuration is required; as soon as you reboot into your on-disk Solaris, you can use the `pkg` command to install extra packages, or package sets, presuming that you have Internet connectivity and DNS configured properly. Note that you can always set your DNS server to be Google's public server, 8.8.8.8, if you at least have IP routing working properly.

It is thus trivial to *add* packages to the very small `solaris-auto-install` package set once it is installed (for example, if you wish to augment it up to the `solaris-large-server` installed package group). However, there is no simple way to downgrade from `solaris-server-large` to a smaller package grouping. Because of this you may wish to have your standard installation CD be the smaller AI one, if you plan on doing a lot of bare-metal installs via CD rather than over the network.

 If you are going to invoke an install program manually, you probably want to use `text-install`. The `auto-install` program likes to have certain prerequisites around. If you have those, then you probably don't want to be wasting your time doing manual installs in the first place.

Text Install image

The Text Install image will skip the GRUB menu entirely, unless you press *Esc* within 5 seconds. Don't panic! Unlike the default AI installer, you will be given a chance to drop out to a shell prompt soon after you set the keyboard type and language preferences.

If you allow it to proceed, it will continue to invoke its local `text-install` script, which will give you a somewhat standard-looking Solaris Text Install sequence.

The initial questions will be the usual choice of primary language, and so on. You can bail out cleanly to a shell prompt or officially start the installer, and eventually get to the selection of computer name and network connection. (Note the *Common traps and pitfalls* section in this chapter.)

This part gets a little weird and nonstandard. Unlike every other part of the installer, you have to press the down arrow key, and highlight the networking choice you want, but then press *F2* instead of *Enter*.

Keep going and eventually, you will get the `group/system/solaris-large-server` set of packages installed to your hard drive, which is currently up to 462 packages. You are not given a choice of which packages to install at the initial install time.

If you would rather install a smaller set of packages from media, you should use the AI image, but manually run the `text-install` program from a shell prompt.

Text Installer does AI too

It is technically possible to use the Text Installer ISO to do AI style installs. However, you have to jump through quite a few hoops if you do not have a custom manifest all set out.

First, you must manually drop into a shell, and then call `auto-install -m some-manifest.xml`. If you do not have a custom one written, you may use the default one in `/usr/share/auto_install/manifest/default.xml`.

This is required because the Text Installer image does not come with the "find manifest automatically" services, aka the `manifest-locator` and `auto-installer` services, automatically enabled. These are mentioned in more detail in the *AI installer client-side services* section of this chapter. You may wish to manually enable them with `svcadm` if you do not wish to manually pull in and invoke a manifest as described previously, and you have the server side already configured appropriately.

There are some important things to note about the `auto-install` program on the Text Install image:

1. It will give you the `solaris-large-server` package set, unless you tell it to use a different manifest file. If you wish for it to install a different package group, you can edit the manifest, and/or copy it to a local HTTP location, and tell it to use that.

2. By default, it will point you at `pkg.oracle.com` for its repository. This is set in the manifest file.

3. Normally, the `text-install` program cheats and just copies its own image files with `cpio` to the disk, rather than doing an official `pkg install` type operation. If however, you use AI, it will use the standard `pkg` mechanisms. Therefore, networking is required if you choose to invoke `auto-install`.

If you don't want to install multiple (more than 5?) instances of Solaris, you probably don't need to read any further in this chapter, other than potentially the *Common traps and pitfalls* section at the end.

Automated Install image

The AI image media is targeted at organizations that have large numbers of machines, but for some reason cannot boot their machines directly from DHCP. (If you can boot from DHCP, why would you want to go running around putting DVDs in every machine?) It is also of interest if you want the smallest on-disk footprint installed. In this case, you can boot from the AI image, but skip to shell and manually use the text-install program.

If you boot from the AI image, you will first see a standard GRUB menu with seven choices, looking similar to the following:

```
Oracle Solaris 11 Install custom

Oracle Solaris 11 Install

Oracle Solaris 11 Install custom ttya

Oracle Solaris 11 Install custom ttyb

Oracle Solaris 11 Install ttya

Oracle Solaris 11 Install ttyb

Boot from Hard Disk
```

For the most part they are self explanatory, allowing you options to have the console be one of the serial ports, or normal, or opt out to boot from the local disk. The three prompts with "custom" might be better labeled "interactive".

In contrast, the near-identical three prompts without the "custom" tag, will not ask any questions whatsoever. They will presume default answers to all questions and do a completely hands-off install.

If you choose the custom option, it will prompt you for the URL of an optional override for the default manifest. Either way, working networking is expected for an AI type of install; although you can drop out of a "custom" install and install directly from the media if you wish.

Getting a shell prompt from AI image

The AI installer does not normally give you a shell prompt. If you wish to avoid it attempting to reinstall to your disk, you should remove the "install" boot time option before fully booting into the OS. In SPARC, this is done by simply typing `boot cdrom`, instead of `boot cdrom - install`. In x86, you must use `e` to edit your chosen GRUB line to remove `install=true` from the kernel line.

Once you have done this, even though it may prompt you about a default manifest, it should go no further than that.

Speed of AI installer

It should be noted that the AI installer will likely be either somewhat slower or significantly slower than the Text Installer, depending on your network speed. It seems to first download the entire set of packages before installing, rather than doing both in parallel. It also may seem to sit doing nothing for several minutes. In contrast, the Text Installer starts copying to the disk right away, and tends to give better progress reports.

Potential problems specific to AI install

If you have a slow DHCP server, or even possibly a slow DNS server, this may result in a fatal error for the AI. It may complain that `pkg.oracle.com` is unreachable. Or the problem may be that the image has a misconfigured the `nsswitch.conf` entry for hosts, as follows:

```
hosts: files
```

Thankfully, all of the fore mentioned errors are recoverable. Log in as user `root`, password `solaris`, then fix what is required.

> If you are attempting to install to a VM, you might try to just increase the size of the emulated disk before you try these fixes. I found that certain types of errors just disappeared when I increased the disk size to 7 GB. Yes, the Oracle FAQ claims the AI installer can work for something as small as 2.5 GB. However, I suspect that is only if you configure it with a custom teeny-tiny manifest, or run the `text-install` command. In contrast, the default template seems to really want at least 7 GB of disk space.

As we will discuss in *Chapter 3, Sysadmin Configuration Differences*, fixing `nsswitch.conf` is not done in the same way as in earlier versions of Solaris. After editing the file, you must run `nscfg import -f name-server/switch`.

Alternatively, you can skip the `vi` and `import` steps by a little hardcoding of /etc/hosts.

```
echo 127.254.56.21 pkg.oracle.com >>/etc/hosts
```

After you have fixed all networking issues (one way to verify this is by `wget pkg.oracle.com`), you can then manually invoke the AI install command, as described in the next section.

Overview of how AI install works

Before using the Automated Installer (AI), it's a good thing to start with a basic understanding of how the AI functions work at a high level.

At a high level, it takes a manifest and profile to determine which packages get installed, and what the identification of the system will be like. This is somewhat similar to the old jumpstart flow — which used a profile rather than a manifest — and a `sysidcfg` file instead of what is now called a profile.

There the resemblance mostly ends. Oracle has extensively changed the means by which the two pieces of information get to the system, and also how their contents are selected.

In the prior Solaris versions, a jumpstart client system downloaded and examined a rules file to find the best match for itself. It then read the matching profile to determine what its disk layout should be, which packages should be installed, and so on.

Oracle has now made this sort of thing a database-driven operation, albeit a simpler database than Oracle Enterprise. There is a special service tasked with providing a target system with a manifest and a profile, based on various levels of criteria.

First, there is the **service name**. This can be specified or overridden by the client. In theory it could be used very flexibly; but in practice, every service name ends up with its own OS boot image, so it might be better named (or at least thought of) as **target OS version**.

Next, there is the **manifest**. As mentioned previously, this determines almost everything about what packages go on disk, as well as the disk layout, and so on. It is entirely up to the server as to which manifest the client receives (if the client is honest about itself at least). Customization of manifests for different install types is commonly done by hand-editing XML.

Lastly, there is the **profile**. This determines the system identity. This is exactly the information generated by the new `sysconfig` command, and in fact that is the command you would normally use to generate it.

AI installer client-side services

Normally, the AI image automatically starts the following two services on the client after boot time:

```
svc:/application/manifest-locator:default
svc:/application/auto-installer:default
```

If you boot without the install option enabled or if they fail, the services may be left in a "disabled" or "maintenance" mode. Unfortunately, once you log in, you may or may not be able to restart the service. The good news is however, that it is not a true continually running service. It is the SMF-hacked equivalent of a hook in /etc/rc2.d/S00xxx. So you have a choice of either manually enabling them with svcadm, or directly invoking the install command that the service would normally start as follows:

```
auto-install -m /system/volatile/ai.xml
```

This file does not initially exist. In a fully-default install, the contents of this file are identical to /usr/share/auto_install/default.xml, so the simplest method to get a default AI install rolling again, is as follows:

```
auto-install -m /usr/share/auto_install/default.xml
```

Alternatively, download or create a custom manifest file as needed.

It should be noted that the default manifest for the AI image installs the set of packages known as the svc:/group/system/solaris-large-server group, which has 462 packages.

So, don't panic if you happen to use pkg list from the OS you boot into for the installer image. Even though it only shows packages contained in svc:/group/system/solaris-auto-install, which contains 335 packages, it will install any grouping you like from the network repository.

Manifest-locator service

The manifest-locator service, svc:/application/manifest-locator, is relatively simple. It contacts the install service, identifies which service name it is interested in, and what it believes its own hostname, IP, and basic characteristics are. It then saves the manifest and profile returned to it to /system/volatile/ai.xml and /system/volatile/profile/### respectively.

It knows what install server/service to connect to, via the install_svc_address and install_service properties provided through either the GRUB menu kernel line, or the wanboot system.conf file provided to the client. As a matter of curiosity, at the lowest level it tends to call the following command:

```
ai_get_manifest -s x.x.x.x:5555:default-(sparc/i386) -o /system/volatile/
ai.xml -p /system/volatile/profile
```

Auto-installer service

The auto-installer service, `svc:/application/auto-installer`, is not any more complicated than the manifest-locator service.

It first checks to see if the "install" keyword was provided at boot time, and if not, it exits.

Otherwise, it is hardcoded to look in `/system/volatile/ai.xml` and the `/system/volatile/profile/` directory, for a manifest and profile to use for installation.

It is good to know this for two reasons: first of all, because you can manually copy over the relevant files to their respective places, and then restart only the auto-installer svc if desired. Secondly, because it is possible to skip restarting the service, and just directly call the same program the service does, with the same arguments.

```
auto-install -m /system/volatile/ai.xml -c /system/volatile/profile
```

AI installer server-side services

An AI install server usually provides a source of manifests and profiles over the network to AI clients, managed by `installadm`. In addition, it can be a source of packages. It may serve a copy of the Oracle packages, or extra packages, or a combination of both.

Serving packages is done by creating or copying an IPS repository. Once this is created, it can be shared through either an SMF `svc:/application/pkg/server` instance, or through plain old NFS. For more details refer *Chapter 1, IPS - The Image Packaging System*.

Once you have your own repository, you can either replace the existing Oracle entry in the relevant manifests, or augment it by adding your own in addition to it. The section in the manifest is as follows:

```
<publisher name="solaris">
    <origin name="http://pkg.oracle.com/solaris/release"/>
</publisher>
```

Network bootstrap process details

Now that the client-side details have been mentioned, you may be interested in the specifics of the client/server bootstrap interactions. The actual setup of this aspect of things is now primarily handled by `installadm`, covered a little further on.

Keep in mind that the initial bootstrap process for network installation for SPARC versus x86 is still very different for each architecture. The backend configuration is new, but still unified for both of them. However, a summary of each follows.

SPARC, wanboot, and DNS

SPARC still uses wanboot at the lowest level. The official Oracle method says that you must use DHCP boot, but whether you boot from media, or directly from network, it still basically just hooks into wanboot as its first stage.

The additional benefit from booting the first stage through DHCP is that it picks up DNS information. In theory, they could have made it pick up DNS from other means, but they have not chosen to do that at this time. This is only a problem if you attempt to use the default manifest, since it references `pkg.oracle.com` by name.

If you simply make your own manifest (or edit the default) to reference the package repository by IP address, AI installs will work just fine without DHCP.

PXE boot and x86

The Solaris 11 x86 net boot sequence is fairly similar to the previous one. You must configure a DHCP server to point the target machine at the `tftpboot` server with an appropriate PXE binary, to bootstrap everything else. If you use the Solaris bundled DHCP (which is now ISC DHCP), the `installadm` tool can actually do this for you with its `create-client` subcommand.

Installer arguments such as the `install_svc_address`, `install_service`, `install_debug`, and `install` flag itself get passed in on the GRUB kernel line, rather than in wanboot's `system.conf` or from the `ok` prompt.

One noticeable difference among the similarities is how the `install` and `install_debug` flags get passed in on **SPARC** versus **x86**.

```
SPARC
boot cdrom - install install_debug
x86 (in menu.lst)
kernel /platform/.... -B install=true,install_debug=true,install_svc_
address=...
```

For SPARC, it should be noted that primarily just the `install` and `install_debug` flags get passed from the `ok` prompt. Other properties get themselves set in the wanboot file of `system.conf`. Normally, you will no longer edit those files directly, but let `installadm` handle it.

Setting up a local install server with installadm

The `installadm` command is Oracle's new admin utility for system installation related issues. It consolidates and replaces things such as the old `setup_install_server` and `add_install_client` scripts.

It is surprisingly easy to install the base requirements for a local network-based install server.

```
// if you dont have installadm already, first do "pkg install installadm"
ARCH=i386 #or sparc
installadm create-service -n $ARCH -a $ARCH
// If you do not want it going under /export/auto_install/$ARCH,
// use -d /export/whereyouwantit
```

With no other options given, this will download a special package named `install-image/solaris-auto-install`. This is an imaged version of all of the packages in the group `solaris-auto-install`, suitable for a network Boot Environment. Basically, this is the set of files on the AI image. When booted off it, almost anything that applies to booting from that physical media will also apply for this net booted image.

Note that this is the smallest possible supported package set for a Solaris installation. This package group has even fewer files than `solaris-small-server`.

Side effects of installadm create-service

In addition to downloading the required packages, the previous command will have a few side effects:

1. It will start a **tftp** server with a root directory of `/etc/netboot`. Curiously, this is true for SPARC, even though it does not use **tftpboot** for first stage boot any more. Even for DHCP booting, you are now supposed to set the **boot file** to be the URL to the install server, just as you would set `file=http:...` in network-boot arguments for wanboot. For some reason, tftp does get used for loading other things later in the boot process, even for SPARC.

2. It will start the service `svc://system/install/server:default`. This is an Apache server, but with some special extra configs running on port 5555. See `/var/installadm/ai-webserver/ai-httpd.conf` if you want full details, or if you wish to change the port.

The following are some points of interest for the `install-server httpd` instance:

- The default docroot is `/var/ai/image-server/images` if you feel like stashing extra things in there, or if you just want to poke around.

- Install manifests are referenced from `(docroot)/(servicename)` — `/var/ai/service/(servicename)/AI_data`. This will be relevant to you, if you start looking at i386 GRUB menu options. When you see examples such as `kernel ..,install_service=namehere`, these top-level subdirectories are what it really refers to. Additionally, if you create custom AI install manifests, these subdirectories are a good place for you to put them. Although there's nothing stopping you from just putting them in the top for your own convenience either.

- The server also acts as the new wanboot server for SPARC Solaris 11. The `installadm` tool outputs the specific URL to use for a boot file when you specify SPARC architecture, which is usually `http://yourhost:5555/cgi-bin/wanboot-cgi`. If you want to keep an existing web start infrastructure around for Solaris 10, see the *Sharing wanboot with Solaris 10 clients* section of this chapter.

Installadm, manifests, and profiles

As mentioned in the *Overview of how AI install works* section, manifests and profiles are the way by which clients are customized. `installadm` is the conduit through which you manage both manifests and profiles on an install server.

Manifests can be thought of as shipping manifests that control what packages get delivered onto a server. They also control where and how they get organized (that is, which separate ZFS filesystems get created).

In contrast, the `installadm` profiles control the identity of a host, similar to that of the old `sysidcfg` files.

Viewing existing manifests and profiles

You can view a list of manifests and profiles using `installadm list`. Be warned however, that the output of this command can vary greatly depending on the flags used.

Command	Description
`installadm list (-n servicename)`	Shows only service names and related information
`installadm list -m (and/or) -p`	Shows all manifest and/or profile names, but does *not* show criteria files
`installadm list -n servicename -m (and/or) -p`	Specifying one service name and the relevant additional flag is the only way to view criteria set for manifests and/or profiles under that service name

Configuring a manifest

Start with a manifest such as `/usr/share/auto_install/manifest/default.xml`.

Copy it and customize it by hand-editing as needed. Then, tell `installadm` to match it to your desired machine types. You must specify a service name; I chose `default-sparc` here but it will allow any one that you have created.

```
installadm create-manifest -n default-sparc -f newfile.xml -m newname
((-c criteria) or (-d))
```

Think of a manifest entry as similar to a line in the old jumpstart rules file. It only makes sense to have one line with "any" as the rule target, but you can have many of them with more refined filters. Similarly, you can have only one default manifest, created with `-d`, but you can create others with more specific filters.

In `installadm` these filters are called **criteria**. You may associate a manifest with one or more combinations of the following criteria:

```
mac ipv4 platform arch cpu network mem zonename
```

Do note that manifest names should be unique. If you leave out the `-m` flag, it will take its name from the filename supplied by `-f`, truncating any `.xml` suffix.

However, you may sometimes wish to reuse the same manifest file for multiple invocations. In this case, it is important to use `-m` to change the name associated in the database for it.

Dynamically generated manifests

Just as it was possible to have a dynamically generated jumpstart rules profile, it is possible to have a dynamically generated AI manifest. Be aware that the hoops to jump through are a bit more complicated. However, registration of a script to do so is relatively easy, you specify it with -f in the same way you would add a regular file. However, you do not get to just print your desired output to stdout. Your script must interact with the aimanifest program.

The procedure for doing so is probably more involved than should be described in this abbreviated chapter. If you are interested in doing so, you should probably refer to the manpage, and if possible, also the full Oracle *E21798* document.

Configuring a profile

To associate a profile within an installadm service, use the following steps:

```
sysconfig create-profile -o /tmp/profilename
//(then answer typical install time "host/network/nameservice" questions)
installadm create-profile -n (servicename) -f /tmp/profilename
```

These steps will then copy the XML in the profile file and associate it with the given servicename. By default, it will be given the same name as the name of the file, which in this case is profilename.

You can only have one active default manifest and one default profile under any one given service name (aka target OS version). However, you can add more of them if you add associated filters, aka criteria.

The create-profile subcommand takes the same list of criteria that create-manifest allows, with the addition of one more allowed criteria keyword.

```
-c hostname=...
```

Templates for profiles

There is a limited capability to use templating for profiles. You can use certain magic variables in a profile. The most useful ones are:

```
${{AI_IPV4}} ${{AI_HOSTNAME}} ${{AI_MAC}} ${{AI_ZONENAME}} ${{AI_
NETWORK}}
```

However, these variables are limited in functionality. They are not substituted at client install time but only when you run installadm.

Thus, if you have the following line in your profile:

```
<propval name="nodename" value="${{AI_IPV4}}"/>
```

And you then run the following command:

```
installadm create-profile -n default-sparc -f profile.tmpl -c
ipv4=1.2.3.4 -p templated
```

You will get a single instance of a profile named `templated`, with the `ipv4` value hardcoded in the `installadm` database entry for the profile.

Note that if you use a particular magic variable, you must define a value for the type the variable represents when you create a profile definition. If you attempt to create it as defined without defining the `ipv4` value, it will complain about an invalid value in the template. `installadm` will not allow `${{AI_IPV4}}` as valid text into its internal database.

Even with these limitations, this is potentially useful enough to use templating in a widespread fashion. However, if you use more than one `templated` parameter (which you sort of have to as you must give values for the hostname, IP address, and default route in the profile), this can lead to a certain amount of ugliness when it comes to reviewing them.

Every criteria you specify for a profile shows up in the output of `installadm list` `-p`. You may not want to redundantly see both the IP address and the hostname linked to a particular profile. To avoid this issue, you can substitute values for `templated` variables via environment variables.

So if you have used both `AI_HOSTNAME` and `AI_IPV4` in a profile template, you may use it in the following way:

```
export AI_IPV4=1.2.3.4
```

```
installadm create-profile -n default-sparc -f profile.template -c
hostname=my-client   -p my-client
```

Similarly, if you would rather trigger the `templated` profile from IP address, but skip the hostname being redundantly shown in the `installadm` list output, use the following command:

```
export AI_HOSTNAME=my-client
```

```
installadm create-profile -n default-sparc -f profile.template -c
ipv4=1.2.3.4   -p my-client
```

Client registration via installadm create-client

There is an additional subcommand to the `installadm` command that is meant to be used on a per-client basis: The `create-client` subcommand. This primarily registers a specific MAC address. It is basically a convenience command to register a specific host in DHCP for x86, or to set up a specific wanboot alias at the top level of `/etc/netboot` that is a `symlink` to the generic real configuration.

For SPARC, you are probably better off just using the profile mechanisms. It may be more useful in the x86 realm as a DHCP assistant type interface, as long as you are running the Solaris DHCP on the same server as your `installadm` server.

Manifests and profiles for zones

It is possible to automatically create and configure zones, either at the installation of the global zone, or at a later time by use of manifests and profiles. For the all-at-once approach, you need only add a single line per zone to the top-level manifest, at the end of your `ai_instance` section:

```
    <configuration type="zone" name="zone1"
     source="http://server/zone1/config"/>
 </ai_instance>
```

This will trigger the initial `zonecfg` creation of `zone1`. However, you must also take a few more steps to tell it what to put in the zone, just as you have to follow an invocation of `zonecfg (create)` with `zoneadm install`.

First, you must create a manifest suitable for the zone. The best place to start is probably the provided one at:

`/usr/share/auto_install/manifest/zone_default.xml`

Then, match it up to your system(s) with `installadm`, with the `zonename` criteria as follows:

`installadm create-manifest -n default-sparc -c zonename=zone1 -m zone1 -f /path/to/xml`

In a similar way it is possible to predefine a profile for a zone, rather than having it prompt via `sysconfig` at first boot for its hostname and so on.

`installadm create-profile -n default-sparc -c zonename=zone1 -p zone1 -f /path/to/xml`

Sharing wanboot with Solaris 10 clients

It is technically possible to share an install server between Solaris 10 and 11 wanboot clients. This is rather important due to the fact that the wanboot-cgi script is hardcoded to use /etc/netboot as its base configuration directory, so it is not possible to run two different versions of it on different ports.

The key component to success for sharing is at the wanboot.conf level. Make sure that each client gets served the appropriate boot_file and root_file parameters. Possibly the easiest strategy is as follows:

Leave the default wanboot configuration to be set to Solaris 10 installs. This means that /etc/netboot/wanboot.conf and /etc/netboot/system.conf are configured for Solaris 10.

Then, for each of your Solaris 11 SPARC clients, run the following command:

```
installadm create-client -e yo:ur:ma:c:ad:dr -n default-sparc
```

This will make an individual top-level symlink in /etc/netboot for the client, similar to how add_install_client used to make symlink in /tftpboot.

The one problem you may run into when using Solaris 10 jumpstart through a Solaris 11 wanboot server is that it may ignore the hostname value you set in network-boot arguments, in favor of what the wanboot server thinks the hostname is, based on a DNS lookup on its IP address.

Common traps and pitfalls

Either just before the install to disk happens or just after reboot, if you used the AI installer, you will be prompted for the various typical sysconfig questions, if you have not preconfigured the system. The prompts seem very similar to the old OS ones, so it is easy to get caught by one of the following issues:

1. Don't choose **Automatically** for your networking type choice, unless you are installing to a laptop or workstation. This choice used to mean simply use DHCP for networking. Unfortunately, it now has the additional meaning of locking you into a netadm profile. This will make it impossible to make permanent changes to networking until you disable it. See *Chapter 4, Networking Nuts and Bolts*, for more details.

2. Don't set up a user account if you want to use root directly. The installer will prompt you for a root password, and also a user account name and password. If you create a user account through this menu option, it will then make the root account unusable except for **role** purposes. This means you will no longer be able to directly log in as root.

While installing to a virtual machine, you must make the disk large enough, or else the install will crash with so much output that you may miss the single line mentioning that the target disk is too small. I recommend no smaller than 6 GB for AI install, or 5 GB for a Text Install. Yes, that's right, the smaller ISO image demands a larger target drive for some reason if you use it through the Automated Install methods.

As an alternative to manually setting up your VM by booting from an ISO image, you could just directly download the VirtualBox VM images that Oracle provides. There is a link to the VM images page under `http://www.oracle.com/technetwork/server-storage/solaris11/downloads/`.

If you choose the **import appliance** option of VirtualBox, this should use the preconfigured settings provided by Oracle, so you will have no worries there. There is also a USB flash drive image you may use from the previous `oracle.com` URL.

If there was an existing ZFS rpool on the disk, it may get automatically mounted under `/a`, which will cause problems to an install. In that case, you will need to run `zpool export rpool` before running `auto-install`.

If for some reason things go very wrong with one of the two install images, you may get to a point where it does not accept the `root` and `solaris` user and passwords. In this case, you might try the fallback of `jack` and `jack`. This is a user level account that also has sudo access.

Solaris 11 release version versus support version

The default Oracle `pkg` repository is `http://pkg.oracle.com/solaris/release`. This is a relatively open repository by design. Oracle allows almost everyone to use base Solaris 11 for almost any reason except for "production use".

If for some reason you end up in a state with no repository configured for your Solaris 11 machine, you can point your `pkg` configuration at that URL, and be able to install packages from the most recent full Solaris 11 release. However, there are no updates or patches.

Configuring your system to use it is fairly easy; you can use the following command:

```
pkg set-publisher -g http://pkg.oracle.com/solaris/release solaris
```

The final argument signifies a "publisher", so normally it would be `something.com`. Unfortunately, Oracle decided to break its own rules for this.

It is possible to have multiple publishers configured, similar to the way in which Red Hat users may configure multiple `yum` repositories. The rule is that there can be only one primary repository configured per publisher.

To get patches and updates from Oracle — currently referred to as Support Repository Updates (SRUs) — you must use a different publisher URL for the `solaris` publisher.

To gain access to the non-public URL, you first need to have a valid Oracle support contract. Next, you must use your Oracle online ID to get a key and certificate from `https://pkg-register.oracle.com/`.

When you receive those access keys, you will also receive information on how to reconfigure your system to point at the support repository of `https://pkg.oracle.com/solaris/support`.

Summary

Solaris 11 drastically alters the way in which installation is done. There are now three different methods to choose from (LiveCD, Text Install, or Automated Install), and all of them are considerably different from the old tried-and-tested methods. Not only do you have three different bases to choose from, but you also need to have a basic grasp of the new package tools to examine the results of what you have installed.

If you are looking to just try Solaris 11 out quickly, whether through an x86 VM, or a temporary boot-from-dvd-only experience, or just the quickest and simplest way to get something on disk, then the x86 LiveCD is the best path for you to follow.

If you want something a bit more controllable, with all the knobs to tweak, then follow the text-based install ISO.

If on the other hand, you are looking to set up many Solaris 11 boxes, you should eventually travel the Automated Installer (AI) path. However, it is strongly recommended that you use Solaris 11 for a while via one of the other two methods first. Getting results that you are completely happy with through an AI based install may take days the first time that you try it.

The good news is, once you find the AI recipe that makes you happy, reusing it is a piece of cake! The bad news is, unless you already are a little familiar with Solaris 11, you may not discover you are unhappy with it until a week or two down the line.

Alternatively, as Oracle OpsCenter is now free to use on Oracle hardware, you might use that to do OS deployments and create OS install profiles for you. It does take a considerable amount of up-front learning to use it, not to mention a machine with at least 8 gigabytes of RAM and 200 GB+ of disk space. That being said, the capability of doing bare-metal installs through a GUI-driven environment is well worth the time investment by any serious enterprise. It also adds in free in-depth hardware and OS level monitoring, giving you twice the benefit for your time and effort. More information on this can be found at:

`http://www.oracle.com/technetwork/oem/ops-center/`

3
Sysadmin Configuration Differences

Solaris 11 has significant changes in the way sysadmins interact with it, even in areas that have not changed since Solaris was first released, or even back to SunOS days. This chapter will get you oriented for the new basic day-to-day ways of doing things.

Welcome to the new normal

The OS configuration has moved further towards the *adm tools and away from the traditional "edit a text file" approach. The three areas of configuration difference that a sysadmin will mostly notice are mentioned in this chapter:

- Host identity
- Driver configuration
- Network configuration

There are also a handful of other minor changes mentioned in the *Miscellaneous differences in system-level configuration* section at the end of this chapter.

Host identity: the sysconfig command

Earlier, if a sysadmin didn't feel like editing the handful of host identity-related files manually, there was the sys-unconfig command.

The new, more modern replacement is sysconfig, which contains three modes:

- configure
- unconfigure
- create-profile

sysconfig configure

This mode essentially brings up a standard Solaris 11 initial, manual installation screen. It prompts you for the usual things, such as hostname, network configuration, and also root account information. Once the information is validated, it reconfigures the system.

Warnings

- Your only chance to back out of host-level changes is when the initial "Do you want to continue?" type prompt appears. If you do proceed, it will unconfigure various things on the live system before asking you your preferences for the hostname and so on.
- Regardless of where you start the program, it will start a new process to ask configuration questions on the system console.

The program claims to create /system/volatile/scit_profile.xml when called in the configure mode. Unfortunately, it does not leave the file around after completion.

sysconfig unconfigure

As the name implies, this mode leaves the system in a "prompt for information" type state for reboot purposes. Therefore, be sure you really mean to do this before executing return on the command line.

sysconfig create-profile

By default, this mode asks the same questions as the configure mode, but saves your answers to a profile in /system/volatile/profile/sc_profile.xml, rather than making live changes to the system.

This profile is useful for configuring automated installs in the same way the old sysidcfg file was used. It can also be used to safely configure a system when console access is lost.

In contrast to the normal configure mode, it will continue to run on the same tty directory that you started it from.

The good news is that it is possible to reconfigure a system even if its console is malfunctioning, by the use of this profile (as shown in the following commands). The bad news is that it gives zero feedback while doing so. If you do have an active console, you would note that the login prompt will change to show any new hostname that you have configured.

```
/dev/tty/23# sysconfig create-profile -o ~/new-sys-profile
// (answer questions in text GUI)
/dev/tty/23 sysconfig configure -c ~/new-sys-profile -g system
// (Prompt returned immediately, while system reconfigures silently with
// no feedback)
```

Driver configuration: /etc/driver/drv

Right from the start of Solaris' first release, the kernel driver configuration was handled in an odd location. The driver.conf files were edited under variations of /kernel/drv or /usr/kernel/drv, rather than under the usual /etc tree.

In Solaris 11, the location has finally been standardized to join the rest of the file-based configuration, under /etc. The new official location for the sysadmin-tuned kernel.conf files is in /etc/driver/drv.

It should be noted that most of the default versions of the driver.conf files are still provided in /kernel/drv; however, if you choose to modify them, you should place the modified versions under /etc/driver/drv.

There are two things to note about this new layout that are of benefit:

1. The original and new .conf files are merged. Therefore, you only need to add changes rather than duplicating the whole file.
2. This preserves your system tuning across driver patches and upgrades more cleanly.

In contrast, something that needs to be ignored is the manpage for driver.conf. Unfortunately, as of the 2011/11 release, the manpage has not been updated to mention /etc/driver/drv. However, some documentation on docs.oracle.com does mention it.

Network address configuration: ipadm and dladm

IP address configuration is now primarily handled by /usr/sbin/ipadm. Oracle is trying to consolidate all IP administration into this tool. Manual configuration above the basic physical interface is almost exclusively handled by ipadm, which controls both IP address assignments, as well as TCP and IP tunables, in a consistent and persistent fashion.

Solaris 11 has attempted to virtualize and automate a bundle of assorted sysadmin tasks, one of which is network configuration. It provides a pair of tools named netadm and netcfg, which follow rule sets for automatically and dynamically managing IP addresses. For now, please ignore the commands that we just mentioned. This section primarily addresses the manual configuration of IP addresses via ipadm.

If your host is currently under automatic network address control and you wish to manually set your network information, you will need to use netadm to change your host to manual network mode (which essentially turns it off).

To do this, you need to change the host's **Network Configuration Profile (NCP)** with the following command:

```
// *** WARNING: This will unconfigure all your network interfaces!!
// Even if you put it back to Automatic, it will not immediately fix it.
//   (but zones will not be affected, even by this global zone change)


netadm enable -p ncp DefaultFixed
```

Note that an Automatic NCP is not the same thing as using DHCP. It is possible to use DHCP within the Automatic NCP, but it is also possible to use it using the DefaultFixed profile.

> If you wish to quickly determine which mode you are in (automatic or manual network configuration), run the following command:
>
> ```
> netadm list
> ```
>
> This will either complain that automatic network management is not available, or it will give a few rows of clean information. To move forward with manual settings, you will want to see something such as the following:
>
> ```
> # netadm list
> netadm: DefaultFixed NCP is enabled; automatic network
> management is not available.
> 'netadm list' is only supported when automatic network
> management is active.
> ```

IP configuration

Configuring a host's IP address is no longer done via text files. The old text files, `/etc/hostname.xxx` and `/etc/dhcp.xxx`, no longer even exist.

Even the device name has changed. Now, by default, Solaris uses generically named interfaces, such as `net0`, for the most part. Virtual interfaces have also changed. Rather than being `net0:1`, they can now be referenced by strings, such as `"net0/web-interface"`. (This is not an either/or reference. A literal '/' character is used in network address interface naming now. The end string is technically referred to as an `addrobj` object.)

This is a very nice feature on a host with multiple network addresses. Even the primary IP address for an interface can be given this string-based name, which greatly reduces the "oops, wrong interface!" factor when the time comes to modify them.

If for some reason you need to trace the generic name back to an old style name, you can do so with the following command:

```
dladm show-phys {net0,...}
```

More will be said about the `dladm` command in the *Network layer 2 device configuration* section later in this chapter.

It is technically possible to force the system to use the old physical device style naming for interfaces. However, the process is ugly. The details are therefore not included here.

`/usr/sbin/ifconfig` still does exist; however, it is no longer adequate for complete administration of IP addresses. For one, it only shows the old style, numeric-based virtual interface number scheme. Additionally, the incentive for getting used to `ipadm` is that it has been stated by Oracle that `ifconfig` will be phased out in a future release.

Following is a table of common usage for `ipadm` given by the context of what admins are used to doing with `ifconfig`. There are other options and parameters that can be manipulated via `ipadm`, but the following table contains a comparison of old style and new style IP commands that you most probably care about:

ifconfig	ipadm
`ifconfig -a`	`ipadm show-addr`
`ifconfig plumb net0`	`ipadm create-ip net0`
`ifconfig net0 1.2.3.4`	`ipadm create-addr -T static 1.2.3.4 net0{/id-string}`
`Ifconfig net0 auto-dhcp`	`ipadm create-addr -T dhcp net0{/id-string} {-h hostname}`
`ifconfig net0 up`	`ipadm up-addr net0{/id-string}`
`ifconfig net0`	`ipadm show-addr net0{/idstring}` (for IP information)
	`ipadm show-if net0` (for information on "dhcp or static", and so on)
	`dladm show-link net0` (for lowest level information)
`ifconfig net0 down`	`ipadm down-addr net0{/id-string}`
`ifconfig unplumb net0`	`ipadm delete-ip net0`

If you have more than one active IP address, it is recommended to label each one with a meaningful /id-string attached to it.

IP interface objects

As you may notice, most of the normal `ipadm` commands listed in the previous table deal with an implied `addr` (officially, `addrobj`) conceptual object. Before you can use or even create an IP address, you must, however, first create an intermediary object with the `create-ip` command. This section attempts to put the `create-ip` command into a more understandable context.

IP addresses in Solaris 11 require the creation of a virtual object to the server as a placeholder at the `ipadm` level for any network-related devices visible at the `dladm` level. This is exactly equivalent to the old `ifconfig plumb` command. It initializes some hooks into the physical device, letting the system know that you intend to perform IP-based networking on it. Without this initialization, any/all other `ipadm` commands related to that device will fail.

With that background in mind, it is helpful to consider the `create-ip` command to be a truncated form of something that makes more sense, such as `create-ip-interface`.

Keeping that mnemonic in mind helps to connect the gap left by the fact that to view `ipadm` objects created by the `create-ip` subcommand, you must use the `show-if` (show interface) subcommand. This is unfortunately inconsistent; there is no `show-ip` subcommand to match the `create-ip` subcommand.

IP interface tunables

In addition to the choice of whether to use a simple IP interface object or a multipath one, some tuning knobs have been lifted away from the IP address level of administration and placed into this new interface object. Things such as **Maximum Transmission Unit (MTU)** are now set at this level. The set-ifprop subcommand of ipadm modifies objects created by either create-ip or create-ipmp in exactly the same way.

IP and TCP tunables

In earlier versions of Solaris, network-level tunables such as ip_forwarding and buffer size were handled by using the ndd tool to tweak in-kernel parameters. Some tunables differed slightly in name, depending on the exact low-level kernel driver attached to the network hardware.

In Solaris 11, Oracle has made the administration of network related tunables more consistent. All networking **layer 3** tunables (such as the TCP, UDP, and IP layer) are now handled by a unified admin command called ipadm.

To get a list of all the tunables that ipadm handles, you can use the following command:

```
ipadm show-prop
```

This will give you quite a long list in multiple protocol-based sections. The current protocol sections are icmp, ipv4, ipv6, sctp, tcp, and udp.

You will probably want to view only one section at a time, which you can do cleanly by specifying the desired protocol as an argument. A shortcut for viewing IPv4 and IPv6 parameters together is by specifying the desired protocol simply as ip:

```
ipadm show-prop tcp
ipadm show-prop ip
ipadm show-prop ipv4
```

If you are interested in the value of one specific tunable or property, you must use the -p flag along with the specific protocol you are interested in. For example:

```
ipadm show-prop -p max_buf tcp
```

Note that specifying the protocol is not optional. In the event that you are interested in the same named property across multiple protocols, you must use grep to get a clean output:

```
ipadm show-prop |grep max_buf
```

To set a property, use the `set-prop` subcommand, similar to the specific invocation of the `show-prop` subcommand. (Remember that unlike `ndd`, this will be persistent.)

```
ipadm set-prop -p max_buf=2097152 tcp
```

It is similarly possible to set per-interface properties, rather than per-protocol properties. To do so, use the `show-ifprop` and `set-ifprop` subcommands. The one major difference is that you must specify the protocol when setting values, and you must do it via the `-m` flag:

```
ipadm show-ifprop net0

ipadm show-ifprop -p forwarding net0

ipadm set-ifprop -p forwarding -m ipv4 net0

// If it complains about "persistent operation on temporary object"
// you must also add -t:

ipadm set-ifprop -t -p forwarding -m ipv4 net0
```

Network layer 2 device configuration

The `dladm` command is not strictly a new command in Solaris 11. Most sysadmins will probably have never used it before, since its main use prior to 11 was to configure link aggregation.

In Solaris 11, however, it takes on responsibility as the primary point of layer 2 configuration. A plethora of subcommands have been added to it, related to Wi-Fi devices, virtual devices (VNICs and Etherstubs), InfiniBand, IP tunnel endpoints, VLANs, and bridge devices. The manpage has grown from around 600 lines to over 5,000 lines. For more details on its new capacities, you should read *Chapter 4, Networking Nuts and Bolts*, and/or the new manpage.

One minor yet useful point of information to anyone who actually used the command previously is that the `show-dev` subcommand has now been renamed to `show-phys`. Additionally, while the `show-linkprop` command has superficially the same syntax in Solaris 11, the output has vastly increased to cover 58 or more separate tunables that were previously handled via `ndd`.

Wireless configuration: Stick to the GUI if you can

In the unlikely event that you are configuring a wireless networking device manually, you will need to use `ipadm` in conjunction with another `adm` tool: `dladm` (Data Link Administration).

Normally, if you are using wireless networking, you would be on a laptop. If so, you would be better off using the automatic network configuration tools, aka NWAM, via the GNOME network GUI. It has a very functional Wi-Fi configuration tool built in, similar to what you will experience on a laptop running Red Hat and GNOME. However, for completeness' sake, and possibly to aid in debugging, here we will configure wireless networking manually on Solaris 11 using the `dladm` and `ipadm` commands.

Unfortunately, this is one area where the new generic naming of interfaces does not normally come into play. Because of this, the first step is to find the name of your wireless network interface. Whenever we wish to deal with physical network device names, we will usually use the `dladm` command. In this case, the specific usage we need, is:

```
dladm show-link
```

We shall pretend that we found an interface named `wifi0`, and continue to set it up:

```
ipadm create-ip wifi0
dladm scan-wifi
dladm connect-wifi {-e ESSID} {other security options}
ipadm create-addr -T dhcp wifi0
```

The following commands are what you need to display the status of your Wi-Fi connection, and how to disable it manually if you wish:

```
dladm show-wifi
dladm disconnect-wifi
```

Miscellaneous differences in system-level configuration

Certain things that used to be in files have been moved into the SMF repository of properties and services.

Some have specialized tools to assist in administration. However, some rely only on the basic SMF property tools, such as svcprop and svccfg.

Name service related

The following is a table of "name service" related, legacy file-based information and the corresponding SMF location:

Filename	SMF location
/etc/nsswitch.conf	svc:/system/name-service/switch:default
/etc/nscd.conf	svc:/system/name-service/cache:default
/etc/resolv.conf	svc:/network/dns/client:default
/etc/defaultdomain	svc:/network/nis/domain:default
/var/ldap/*	svc:/network/ldap/client:default

Each of the old-style file's information in the left column can be imported manually into SMF via the nscfg command. It is also possible to do one-shot exports of the information. The sample usage of each action is as follows:

```
nscfg import -f svc:/network/dns/client:default
nscfg export svc:/system/name-service/cache:default
```

The preceding two commands will first trigger the system to update the running DNS hooks in SMF with the current contents of /etc/resolv.conf. Secondly, it will dump the current nscd settings from the SMF database into /etc/nscd.conf.

Either way, the important thing to remember is that the active system services only look at the information in SMF. The only time it will look at the old files in /etc, is when you tell it to explicitly update the SMF database settings with whatever is in the relevant file at the current point in time.

Time zone and language settings

Time zone and language settings were previously set in `/etc/default/init`. This is no longer true.

They are now read from the properties in the SMF container `svc:/system/environment:init`.

To view possible properties to adjust, you may use the following command:

```
svcprop -p environment svc:/system/environment:init
```

Nodename

`/etc/nodename` is no longer a place to set, or even check a host's current hostname. It does not even exist. The equivalent is an `svc` property viewable with the following command:

```
svcprop -p config/nodename  svc:/system/identity:node
```

But you were using `uname  -n` for that sort of information, so you don't care, right?

Summary

This chapter attempts to address some of the more common system administration changes that a sysadmin might encounter and that have new interfaces in Solaris 11. The network-level coverage here is more of a tactical level, rather than an architectural one. For a more in-depth view of the Solaris 11 network tools, and a better understanding of the new network kernel architecture in general, be sure to read *Chapter 4, Networking Nuts and Bolts*.

One thing that is not mentioned, is the day-to-day type operations dealing with ZFS. If you are not already familiar with it, you should also be sure to read *Chapter 6, ZFS – Now You Can't Ignore It!* carefully.

Most other daily sysadmin chores that are not mentioned in this chapter have not changed since Solaris 10.

4
Networking Nuts and Bolts

Basic IP configuration has been addressed in the *Chapter 3, Sysadmin Configuration Differences*. This chapter covers advanced network configurations possible in Solaris 11, along with a more in-depth overview of the changes.

Networking re-architected

Solaris 11 has a vastly redesigned networking infrastructure, both at the kernel level, and at the sysadmin level. It is crucial to understand this redesign.

Therefore, I shall start this chapter with some orientation material.

The following topics are touched on in this chapter:

- Kernel redesign
- Orientation to new Solaris 11 networking
- Interface naming
- NWAM – automatic networking configuration
- IPMP (IP multipathing), tunneling, and VLAN management
- Network resource management (per-interface, flows, and IP QoS)
- Other changes

The changes in Solaris 11 improve both performance, and general manageability. In the manageability department, changes you make with the new tools stay across reboots.

Kernel redesign

Prior to Solaris 11, many, but not all, network drivers took advantage of a common driver framework called the **Generic LAN Driver (GLD)** framework.

Now in Solaris 11, virtually all drivers use GLD Version 3. This has allowed a redesign of the kernel-to-user interface to bring standardization to Solaris networking.

Additionally, a long-standing mandatory kernel intermediary layer, called **STREAMS,** has been stripped out of the required path (although it is still available as an option). This has allowed some performance optimizations that were previously impossible.

Back in 2009, Solaris engineers started work on a new internal kernel network architecture nicknamed "Crossbow". Work on this new design was put into **OpenSolaris,** and thus has seen quite a lot of field testing over its design. Some fruits of this testing and design found their way into Solaris 10, under a nickname of "FireEngine", which improved network performance to some degree. Its biggest improvements were in the realm of multi-CPU handling of network drivers. Compatibility with existing APIs constrained its performance.

In Solaris 11, Crossbow brings this research to its full potential.

Usually, virtualization of physical devices brings a performance penalty, but Crossbow is an exception. To quote its chief architect, Sunay Tripathi, in an OpenSolaris talk back in 2009:

> *"Crossbow is network virtualization and scaling. You don't need to use virtualization parts of Crossbow. OpenSolaris with Crossbow makes Asterisk performance go up 4 times."*

Orientation to new Solaris 11 networking

Networking functionality has now been split into layers, almost similar in some ways to how the old simple method of accessing disks through *disk slices*, got split up by ZFS into pools, mirrors, and the like.

Previously, almost all network configuration in Solaris was done by the physical interface, xyz0, and some permutation of the ifconfig command. Now, however, the multiple personalities of ifconfig, have been divided up into separate commands and layers.

The basic layers can be grouped as follows:

Physical, readonly (dladm)	Data link (dladm)	IP interface (ipadm)	IP "addrobj" (ipadm)
bge0, nxge0, e1000g0, and so on	net0, vlan0, vnic0, aggr0, stub0	net0, (simple case usually should match data link object name), ipmp0	net0/labelhere

To configure an IP address generally requires one item from each column, building step-by-step, from the left-most column, until you get to the right-hand side.

The left-most column is only visible from a global zone, via dladm show-phys. Usually you can completely ignore it, and start at the second data link column. By default, all physical devices get assigned generic data link names that look like net0 or net1.

The most common chain looks like (physical) → net0 → net0 → net0, which of course makes the casual observer wonder why on earth this seems so needlessly complex and redundant. The benefits become obvious as soon as you wish to do more fancy things at the sub-IP level.

For example, you can easily change the underpinnings of a particular IP address, from a single device, to an aggregation of two or more. Similarly, if you have four physical interfaces, and have previously allocated one individually per zone, or per service, you might change your mind later, and reconfigure them to share a 4-device aggregation. You can then choose whether to merely have them share IP addresses on the same *IP interface*, or possibly give them each their own virtual device (aka VNIC) built on top of the aggregation device.

You do have to bring down the interface before reconfiguring lower levels, unless you are adding or removing a member from an interface aggregation.

Interface naming and IP labels

By default, all network interface names visible at the general sysadmin level, are now simply called net0, net1, and so on. The inconsistency of names such as bge0, e1000g0, and ngxe0 are now hidden from view.

If you have different types of physical interface, and you need to know which `netX` name maps to which specific physical name, you can view mappings with:

`dladm show-link`

This command will show you *all* `dladm` level devices, including Virtual NICs and aggregation links. However, if you would like to narrow it down to just the ones associated with physical interfaces, you should use the following command:

`dladm show-phys`

Beyond that, what you most likely care even more about, after the initial setup, is which interface is being used for what purpose. Even more in this era of virtual services and zones, it is nice to know this information per IP address, rather than per interface. To that end, Solaris 11 associates IP address with user-named strings. Now if you are wondering which of your 10 virtual IP addresses is being used by your Apache instance, you no longer have to trace through Apache configs; you can look at the IP related interface `net1/apacheVIP`, rather than `nxge1:4`.

A simple static IP example

A trivial example of configuring a static IP address (whether the first one, or a secondary one on a physical interface) is as follows. This presumes that you already can see the low-level device with `dladm show-phys net0`:

`ipadm create-ip net0`

`//above not necessary if you already have an initial IP assigned for it`

`ipadm create-addr -T static -a local=1.2.3.4/24 net0/newstatic`

Note that the argument `create-ip` must be the exact same name as a `dladm show-link` object. In contrast, the `newstatic` label at the end of `create-addr`, can be almost any text that you wish it to be.

Network infrastructure impact on zones

Because of the forced abstraction of the API that network drivers have to use, it is now possible to allow zones to have 90 percent of the control over their network interface, than a global zone does. Snoop can now be run in zones, even when the zone does not completely *own* the interface. It is possible to create a virtual network device on top of a physical one, and give it an independent MAC address. In that way, it is now possible to give zones their own network interface, even when you only have a single physical interface.

If you configure a zone to have `ip-type=exclusive` (which is now the default), it is possible to allow the zone to set its own IP address(s), from a list of allowable addresses that you set per **net** or **anet** resource.

Furthermore, with the new anet (Automatic network interface) resource, it is possible to allow, or disallow, a zone from changing the Ethernet address of an interface. (So long as they are configured with the new anet resource for networking, rather than the older *net* resource, and/or have IP addresses autoassigned.)

The new anet zone resource enables a sysadmin to give a zone low-level access to a network interface, yet disallow the ability to change the MAC address, and/or the IP address. It is even allowable to grant zone access to multiple pre-assigned IP addresses, without allowing configuration of non-assigned ones.

 In certain situations, it is possible for the child zone to snoop some information from the global, if you do this virtual sharing of a single interface. However, it would only be able to see broadcast type traffic.

NWAM – NetWork AutoMagic

Someone on the Solaris engineering team decided to name this feature, **Network AutoMagic**. But from a server sysadmin perspective, it might perhaps be better named "Never Wake A Monster".

NWAM is primarily useful for people running Solaris on a laptop, who have to deal with wireless in different locations. If you are the *console user* (that is, physically in front of the machine), and within the GNOME-based desktop, you will have a fairly nice tool that allows you to easily configure wireless, and even swap between location-based profiles for other IP needs. In that context, it is fairly useful. If, on the other hand, your systems are servers which ignore DHCP, it is best avoided.

NWAM gets in the way of doing almost anything intelligent or fancy with the normal network control tools `dladm` or `ipadm`. It will cause complaints about "Persistent operation on temporary object". Technically, you can add the `-t` flag to `dladm` or `ipadm`, to make your operation temporary as well, but a major benefit from the new tools is that the changes you make, stick, so why bother?

In theory, NWAM can be used to automagically configure machines using a central-IT controlled set of profiles. However, most people will probably use other means for that sort of thing.

NWAM pitfalls

NWAM has the following drawbacks that need to be understood:

1. You may not realize when you are getting it.

   At initial Solaris install time, if you go through an interactive installation, you will be faced with a choice of automatic or manual networking. It does not say what automatic means, so based on past experience, you may choose this as meaning DHCP. It will indeed go with DHCP; however, if you change your mind later, and try to "un-DHCP" your box, it will fight you and you won't know how or why. There is no indication in `dladm` output or `ipadm` output that the interfaces are being managed by NWAM.

2. It does not play well with others.

   If you disable it, it will unconfigure all the interfaces it has autoconfigured.

   If you re-enable it, it will not automatically recreate them reliably, and there is no obvious way to tell it, "hey, reset everything and start from scratch".

   Not only that, but it is unfriendly on configuring it as well. If you enable, or re-enable, automatic mode, it will unconfigure any interfaces you have made manually. If you suddenly realize your mistake, and say, "oops, go back to manual", it will not restore the configurations it has destroyed.

The most important thing you need to know, that is not mentioned in the manpage, or in listings of profiles of `netadm list`, is how to turn it off. You do this by enabling a different profile. Annoyingly, while `netadm` lists `Automatic` as a known profile (when NWAM is enabled), it *does not* acknowledge the existence of the profile `DefaultFixed`. So don't forget it!

```
netadm enable -p ncp DefaultFixed
// Take back control of your network interfaces!
```

This changes your Network Configuration Profile (`ncp`), from `Automatic` (or anything else), to `DefaultFixed`, which is actually a synonym for "Disable NWAM completely". As previously mentioned, it will unconfigure all interfaces at this time, so don't do this while anything important is running!

Sneaking around NWAM with VNICs

If, for some reason, you wish to keep NWAM enabled, but also have an additional permanent static IP address, there is a simple way to do this. NWAM ignores VNICs. So, it is possible to do the following:

```
dladm create-vnic -l net0 vnic0
ipadm create-ip vnic0
ipadm create-addr -T static -a local=1.2.3.4 vnic0/permaddress
```

Using NWAM via GUI

As mentioned, for desktop users, there is an NWAM GUI, which makes switching between NWAM-recognized locations relatively easy. You can invoke it using three different methods:

- From the desktop menus, navigate to **System | Administration | Network**
- Via the **network-status** icon on the top right of the desktop screen
- From the command line via `nwam-manager-properties`

The GUI functions similarly to other popular OS's network location tools. It lets you create a location-oriented profile with your preferred name (for example, "Home" or "Office"), and then allows you to specify various preferred configurations for your wireless and wired connectivity.

For a complete step-by-step guide to use NWAM, see *Chapter 5, NWAM – Auto-reconfiguration*.

IPMP – IP multipathing

IP multipathing is a configuration that allows an IP address to automatically failover between two or more physical network interfaces. Prior versions of Solaris did already have IPMP support, but it was a bit hacky. It involved using `ifconfig` to assign two or more interfaces to a *group*, and then basically hoping the kernel did a good job from there. It was then up to the kernel to plumb and unplumb a secondary IP address (such as `bge0:1`) from one physical interface or another.

IPMP support in Solaris 11 is much more refined. The floating IP is given its own persistent, virtual object, at the same level as any other IP object at the `ipadm` layer. This then allows you to apply persistent tuning options to it.

There is also a new tool specifically written to monitor IPMP; predictably, it is called `ipmpstat`.

Setting up IPMP

Before you can set up a multipath IP object, you first have to set up underlying regular IP objects and interfaces with their own IP addresses (so that they can ping-test to validate the operation). Let's say you have already done this with interfaces `net0` and `net1`. To take advantage of that with a highly available IP address on top of that, use the following steps:

```
ipadm create-ipmp ipmp0
ipadm add-ipmp -i net0 -i net1 ipmp0
ipadm create-ip -T static -a local=1.2.3.4 ipmp0/redundantVIP
```

 You cannot have a physical interface belong to more than one IPMP group. If you attempt to add one to a second group, it will silently remove it from its original one. So, take care when adding interfaces!

If you have a third functional physical interface available to you, you may choose to add it as a `standby` interface, by using the following steps:

```
ipadm add-ipmp -i net2 ipmp0
ipadm set-ifprop -p standby=yes net2
```

Don't forget to use the `ipmpstat` command to check on the status from time to time. See the manpage for more information.

Link aggregation

Link aggregation, aka "trunking", is similar, yet different to IP multipathing (IPMP). Both actually let you increase outbound bandwidth by spreading it across multiple links. Both give you a measure of automatic failover support. However, only link aggregation lets you spread inbound bandwidth across multiple links.

That's the good news. The bad news is link aggregation has some important limitations that, while they may not be a problem in "small to midsize" shops, can be a problem in enterprise level endeavors.

Link aggregation uses the **IEEE 802.3ad** protocol, sometimes known as LACP. This makes it an Ethernet-only solution. An even stronger limitation is that all the links that are aggregated together must be on the same switch.

In contrast, IPMP, can be used across truly redundant, separate switches. Furthermore, as it is an *IP-level* solution, rather than a *link-level* solution, it can be used on top of alternative transports such as InfiniBand.

The bonus good news, for people who want it all, is that IPMP is so flexible that it can even be used on top of link aggregation in Solaris 11. So if you have enough hardware to throw at it, have a blast!

To set up link aggregation between `net0` and `net1`, use the following (note that this is link-level, therefore, it uses `dladm`, rather than `ipadm`):

```
dladm create-aggr -l net0 -l net1 aggr0
ipadm create-ip aggr0
ipadm create-addr -T static -a local=1.2.3.4 aggr0/buffbandwidth
```

To go hog-wild, the full IPMP over LACP setup would look something like the following:

(Presuming that `net0`/`net1` are on one switch, and `net2`/`net3` are on a different one.)

```
dladm create-aggr -l net0 -l net1 aggr0
dladm create-aggr -l net2 -l net3 aggr1
ipadm create-ip aggr0
ipadm create-ip aggr1
ipadm create-addr -T static -a local=1.2.3.4 aggr0/buffbackend0
ipadm create-addr -T static -a local=1.2.3.5 aggr1/buffbackend1
ipadm create-ipmp ipmpULTIMATE1
ipadm add-ipmp -i aggr0 -i aggr1 ipmpULTIMATE1
ipadm create-addr -T static -a local=1.2.3.100 ipmpULTIMATE1/offTheHOOK
```

VNIC – Virtual NIC

Prior to Solaris 11, it was always possible to add a virtual, or secondary IP address to a network interface, such as bge0:1 on top of bge0.

Solaris 11 takes things an important step further, by allowing you to encapsulate an IP address within a virtual network interface object. This object can be treated as a first class network entity in its own right. It is possible to run snoop on it. It is also possible to assign it to a zone, and allow the zone to have full access to it, without compromising the security of the physical device, or other VNICs on that device.

You can name a VNIC almost anything you want, as long as you put a number at the end of it. For ease of comprehension, however, you may want to stick to the standard of vnicX.

Sample usage is as follows:

```
dladm create-vnic -l net0 vnic1
ipadm create-ip vnic1
ipadm create-addr -T static -a local=1.2.3.9/24 vnic1/extraIP
snoop -d vnic1
```

As mentioned, snoop will pick up traffic related to 1.2.3.9, and to broadcast traffic, but will not see unicast traffic for other IPs that are not bound to vnic1, even if they share the same physical interface.

It is also possible to assign additional IP addresses to vnic1 with ipadm create-addr.

VNICs are link objects but not physical interface objects. Notice the difference between the two outputs of dladm:

```
# dladm show-link
LINK          CLASS      MTU      STATE       OVER
net0          phys       1500     up          --
vlan0         vlan       1500     up          net0


# dladm show-phys
LINK          MEDIA      STATE    SPEED    DUPLEX    DEVICE
net0          Ethernet   up       1000     full      e1000g0
```

It is also possible to create VNICs on top of an aggregation object:

```
dladm create-aggr -l net0 -l net1 -l net2 aggr0
dladm create-vnic -l aggr0 vnic0
dladm create-vnic -l aggr0 vnic1
```

VLAN tagging

VLAN tagging is a network layer 2 standard designed to allow separate Ethernet broadcast domains to coexist safely on a single physical interface or network fabric. Configuring a virtual IP address or virtual network interface with a specific **VLAN ID**, or **tag**, is the way to let the network hardware know which broadcast domain to assign a packet to.

Solaris 10 supported use of VLAN tagging for interfaces; however, the administrative interface was highly ugly. It involved using `ifconfig` to plumb virtual interfaces with mandatory 6-digit numbers.

Solaris 11's unified network interface allows for much cleaner VLAN tagging usage. You can now create a VLAN tagged virtual interface that is a top-level network entity in its own right. Basically, it is a VNIC with a fixed extra attribute, which is the VLAN tag ID. You can give it a custom name to denote that it is not just an ordinary VNIC, but after that, you can treat it as any other VNIC level device. For example:

```
dladm create-vlan -l net0 -v 99 privatevlan1
ipadm create-ip privatevlan1
```

The following command shows a comparison view of the new entity, alongside a regular VNIC:

```
# dladm show-link
LINK            CLASS    MTU     STATE        OVER
net0            phys     1500    up           --
vlan0           vlan     1500    up           net0
privatevlan1    vnic     1500    up           net0
```

IP tunneling

In Solaris 10 and earlier, it was possible to create IP tunnels manually, using `ifconfig`. In Solaris 11, you use the `dladm` and `ipadm` commands. The bad news is the process involves a few more steps. The good news is it is automatically persistent across reboots, and also is more readable, by virtue of the fact that you can *name* the tunnels.

To create an IPv4 tunnel between your own host at `1.2.3.4` and a remote gateway at `5.6.7.8`, use the following sequence of commands:

```
dladm create-iptun -T ipv4 -a local=1.2.3.4,remote=5.6.7.8 tunnelname0

ipadm create-ip tunnelname0

ipadm create-addr -T static -a local=1.2.3.4,remote=5.6.7.8 tunnelname0/
usefulnamehere
```

As you can see, the syntax is fairly similar to VLAN creation. First, the creation of a base-layer kernel object is required, through `dladm`. After that, the IP-level setup via `ipadm` is almost identical to other IP administrative tasks.

Bridging

Bridging is the term used when a device transparently forwards network layer 2 packets from one broadcast domain to another. In essence, it can make the Solaris server act like an Ethernet switch (or in some cases, other layer 2 protocol switches).

 Bridging makes the involved physical interfaces to always run in promiscuous mode, which has the effect of degrading effective interface throughput.

Normally, I would consider bridging on a Solaris box to not be used enough to include here, but the improvements in Solaris 11 are so impressive that they are worth mentioning.

The old way of making a Solaris machine act as a bridge was to set `ip_forwarding=1` on the interfaces you wished, then telling other machines to use the Solaris machine as a bridge, and blindly hope for the best.

The new way is much improved. There are real administrative commands instead of `ndd`, and the OS has been enhanced to properly support the following standard bridging protocols:

Spanning Tree Protocol (STP), **Rapid Spanning Tree Protocol (RSTP)**, and the relatively new TRILL protocol (see `http://tools.ietf.org/wg/trill/`).

To create the default type of bridge, using the STP protocol, use the `dladm` commands in one of the two ways:

```
dladm create-bridge BRIDGENAME
#includes ALL network interfaces
dladm create-bridge BRIDGENAME -l net0 -l net3
# limit to specific interfaces
```

To create it using TRILL protocol, add `-P trill`, or use `dladm modify-bridge ...` on an existing one.

This will start a bridge-specific instance of `/usr/lib/bridged` (or for TRILL, `/usr/lib/trilld`), and an SMF item, `svc:/network/bridge:BRIDGENAME`. It will also create a special virtual device named `/dev/net/BRIDGENAME0`, for various administrative purposes. If you were to run `snoop` on this device, it would only capture incoming traffic.

For TRILL, the results are trivially different. Instead of bridged, an instance of `/usr/lib/trilld` will be started.

Once set up, a bridge is fairly self-maintaining, but it is worth knowing that there are also new bridge-specific tools to monitor its status, by way of the `dladm show-bridge` subcommand combined with various command-line options. See the manpage for full details.

Network resource management

Now, there are three main ways to handle resource management in Solaris 11: by flows, by interface, and by custom Quality of Service rules.

The QoS methods are the most flexible, but also highly complex, and perhaps best avoided unless absolutely necessary.

Related to resource management is knowing just how much data is flowing through the resource. At a coarse level, the `dlstat` command will tell you the amount of data that has been flowing through a low-level physical or virtual interface. Similar to the `iostat` command, it can show you total number of packets since reboot, or you can tell it to report over regular intervals.

At a little more refined level, is the `flowstat` command, mentioned in the *Flow-based resource management* section.

Per-interface management

There are two types of resource management on an `dladm` level interface that are of interest:

- CPU based
- Bandwidth based

Limits are set through interface properties. You could consider them somewhat similar to old ndd-style settings, except that the settings persist across reboots. It is also possible to use them within zones that have *exclusive* use of a network interface, whether physical or virtual.

You can see all possible link properties for a link by `show-linkprop`:

```
dladm show-linkprop net0
```

The following example sets a limit of 3 megabits/sec, and use of a particular CPU Pool set (created by `poolcfg`). It is also possible to bind it to an individual CPU directly, if you do not wish to use pools:

```
dladm set-linkprop -p maxbw=3m,pool=cpupool1 net0
```

Flow-based resource management

A `flow` is a little like running the old trusty `snoop` command. It can be set to look at packets filtered by attributes such as traffic type (`tcp/udp/icmp/etc`), port, source, or destination. The differences from snoop are significant, however.

First and foremost, it is much, much more efficient than snoop. Whereas snoop has to put the interface into promiscuous mode and records all matched packets, flows only count packets (see `flowstat` to view either a total count, or count over time intervals of a created `flow`). This makes flows have almost no performance impact on the system.

Secondly, flows can be used to manage bandwidth!

The following set of commands limits the amount of traffic that can be used for HTTP downloads over the given interface to 1 gigabit/sec. Technically, it can be done all in one line at creation time, but may be a little more readable in two:

```
flowadm add-flow -l net0 -a local_port=80,transport=TCP http-downloads
flowadm set-flowprop -p maxbw=1G http-downloads
// and if you are feeling paranoid, verify the settings:
flowadm show-prop
```

Then, if you are wondering how the traffic is performing over time, you can take a look at it now and again, with `flowstat` giving you a summary interactively, every 30 seconds, or however often you want it to do so:

```
flowstat http-downloads -i 30
```

IP QoS – Quality of Service management

Over time, Solaris has been adding more and more methods of resource management on a server. Solaris 11 has the ability to manage IP traffic bandwidth as a resource. It is now possible to put resource limits on IP use based around typical things such as IP source or destination. In addition, it is even possible to create resource limits on specific users and projects.

IP Quality of Service is managed through the `ipqosconf` command. It is important to note that the command is most likely not installed by default on your machine, so it may be necessary to execute the following command:

```
pkg install ipqos
```

 While IP QoS seems to be an extremely powerful and useful feature, as of early 2012, it is still a little on the bleeding edge. The `ipqosconf` tool has a bad tendency to core-dump while attempting to load a configuration file. Hopefully, this issue will be resolved in future patch levels. However, in the meantime, it may be a better option to use `flowadm`, which has less flexibility, but may be more reliable.

The high level flow for using this tool is as follows:

1. Create one (or more) QoS related configuration files under `/var/ipqos`.
2. Activate it to test it out.
3. Permanently *configure* it into the post-reboot kernel configuration.

Step 1 – Create a temporary QoS configuration file

The Oracle recommended location to create this type of file is under `/var/ipqos`. There does not seem to be anything special about that location. However, Oracle documentation on monitoring and auditing QoS traffic also uses this directory in its examples. (See manpages for `flowacct` and `acctadm`.)

The actual final configuration will be configured and activated via the intermediate file `/etc/inet/ipqosinit.conf`.

If it is present at boot time, it will then be loaded into kernel configuration. In theory, it would only then be possible to edit `/etc/inet/ipqosinit.conf` directly. However, given the newness of the technology, it would be prudent to have the configuration file verified by the official tool before doing something that potentially could take your server off the network after a reboot.

Probably the only reasonably safe alternative would be to dump a *working* current kernel QoS configuration to the file using `ipqosconf -l`.

The specific syntax of a QoS configuration file can get complicated; QoS management is as flexible, and powerful as a firewall configuration, or perhaps even more so. There are examples of various configurations in `/etc/inet/ipqosconf.#.example`.

Step 2 – Activate the QoS rules file

To activate, or *add*, a QoS rules file, use the following command:

```
ipqosconf -a /path/to/file
```

Remember that this immediately activates the configuration.

Step 3 – Permanently configure (-c) it into the post-reboot kernel

This part also has easy syntax. To make your changes stick across reboot, use the following:

```
ipqosconf -c
```

Or, a possible alternative would be as follows:

```
ipqosconf -l >/etc/inet/ipqosinit.conf
```

This is not recommended, however.

Other changes

Other things that have changed in Solaris 11 networking, that we won't go into detail about here, but are worth mentioning briefly:

- The **netcat** utility is now included in Solaris. This is useful for a simple user-level network port redirector. **Wireshark** is also just a `pkg install` away.

- The supported DHCP server for Solaris is now the ISC DHCP server (the most common open source one).

Since this DHCP server is widely known and documented, the only things worth mentioning here are the Solaris specific bits:

New DHCP SMF service FMRIs:

```
svc:/network/dhcp/server:ipv4
svc:/network/dhcp/server:ipv6
```

New DHCP server configuration files:

```
/etc/inet/dhcpd4.conf
/etc/inet/dhcpd6.conf
```

- Solaris 11 supports **Virtual Router Redundancy Protocol (VRRP)**. However, since most readers will probably not want to turn their Solaris box into a router, all that needs to be mentioned here is that there is a single administrative command, predictably named `vrrpadm`.

Summary

Solaris 11 networking administration has changed so much that it is almost like using a different operating system. There are clear benefits from the new admin interfaces, as well as the performance benefits of the kernel rearchitecture. The most important takeaways for the new networking paradigm are to understand what new capabilities are now available and to know which toolsets are most important to use.

First and foremost, remember the following parallel paths for tool chains:

- **NWAM profile-oriented configuration**: `netcfg` and `netadm`. Despite the generic names, these are only for NWAM.
- **Standard sysadmin tools**: `ipadm`, `dladm`, `flowadm`, `flowstat`, and `dlstat`. Remember that `ipadm` and `dladm` only work normally if NWAM is disabled.

Secondly, remember the virtualization and stackability of the new VNIC, VLAN, and `aggr` objects. You can treat any of these types as a first class object, where you can assign exclusive use of them to a zone, including snoop and IP address control. You can also stack an IPMP object on top of a VNIC or VLAN object, on top of an `aggr` object, on top of a real physical object, or any simpler combination that you may wish

5
NWAM – Networking Auto-reconfiguration

Unix sysadmins often joke about using dark magic to keep systems running. Seldom has a product or tool officially had magic in its name however. Oracle seems to have recognized this and mostly refers to it as "Reactive Networking" from Solaris 11.1 onwards.

What is NWAM and how you can use it

NetWork AutoMagic, aka **NWAM**, is an environment that helps you switch between various network-related configurations in one go. It is primarily useful for laptops as well as for mobile computers. It might also potentially be useful for an OS image that was duplicated across many machines that would be expected to configure themselves when turned on in their final deployment location, rather than once at install time.

Most system administrators of server-class hardware will probably choose to use the manual network configuration tools detailed in *Chapter 4*, *Networking Nuts and Bolts*, rather than using NWAM.

Capabilities of NWAM

In the age of almost ubiquitous DHCP, most folks will only need to use the automatic settings. But if you need to integrate with a secure network (or perhaps the problem is a less than secure network), you may wish to make some customizations beyond what the bare DHCP offers you.

NWAM offers a way for an individual user at the console to be able to control almost every network-related aspect of the OS, such as:

- Which network interfaces are active
- Static or DHCP-controlled IP addresses
- Static or DHCP-controlled DNS
- Which naming service to use (NIS, LDAP, or FILES)
- The use of IPSEC policies and keys
- The use of IPfilter and/or NAT

It is also possible to automatically have these settings activated under certain network conditions.

This chapter will deal with the most common interface of NWAM, which is the GUI on a laptop user's desktop. If needed, it can be invoked from the command line as nwam-manager-properties, but normally it will be invoked either from the **Network** menu in **System | Administration** or from the network icon, both of which are shown in the following screenshot:

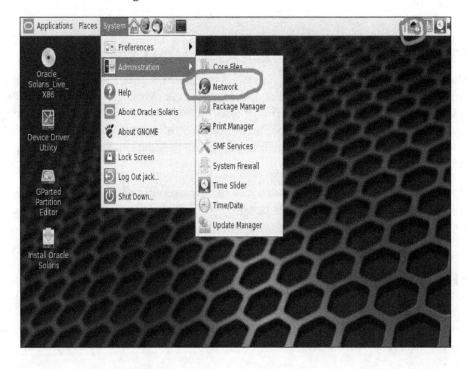

If you hold your mouse over the network icon, you will get a tool tip informing you of the current NWAM configuration.

Clicking on either will bring up the top-level NWAM window in **Connection Status** mode. This shows the interfaces that are currently active, as well as the IP address and speed information (including IPv6 information, if active).

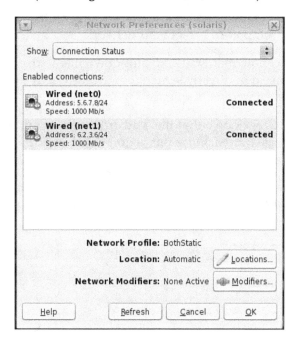

NWAM basic concepts

Before going any further, it is important to understand the three basic components of NWAM, namely **Connections**, **Profiles**, and **Locations**.

Connections

Connections are basically network interfaces. So the default GUI display of **Connection Status** summarizes the current status of the active network interfaces.

Profiles are top-level objects that essentially just determine which network interfaces are active. In and among themselves, they do nothing else. However, it is possible to trigger a change of the **Location** setting based on which Profile has been selected.

Locations are a method of organizing "everything else", such as name services and IP security related settings. They are also the entity level at which you create automated configuration switching rules.

Profiles

To choose the Profile you want active, you must change the top pull-down menu to **Network Profile**, activate the appropriate radio button for your desired profile, and click on the **OK** button at the bottom. Note that clicking on the **OK** button will close the GUI and possibly temporarily reset your network.

It is also important to know that while the pull-down menu displays all the known profiles, you cannot use it to directly switch the currently active profile. You must go through the previously described sequence.

To create a new profile, click on either the **Add** or **Duplicate** button, as appropriate, and change the name as desired. Once this is done, click on the **Edit** button to actually configure your new profile.

First of all, make sure that your desired interfaces, aka *connections*, show up in the list. This is particularly important if you chose to add a new profile since that defaults to not having any interfaces in the profile.

To change this, click on the **Connections** button in the top-right corner, select the interfaces that you wish to activate in this profile, and click on **OK**.

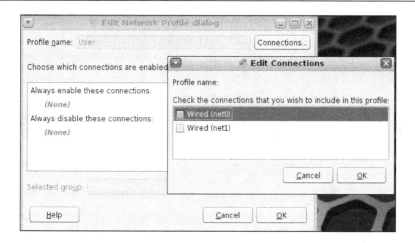

Once you have done this, you may wish to select them in the **Edit Network Profile dialog** window and click on the **Up** button to simplify the display. If they do not appear, you may need to click on **OK** and then re-edit the profile.

Once you have configured the desired network interfaces in a profile, you must go to the top level window to be able to change the settings.

Holding down the top pull-down menu should now show the new profile as well as any interfaces associated with it.

Remember that the pull-down menu does not switch the active profile. So go ahead and use it to select the interface you want, making sure that you choose it under the specific profile you wish to modify.

The following screenshot shows the next section of the GUI which allows you to change the IPv4 and IPv6 addresses for the interface when in the selected profile. It allows you to set them either statically or via DHCP, or have both DHCP and the additional static IP addresses assigned to the interface.

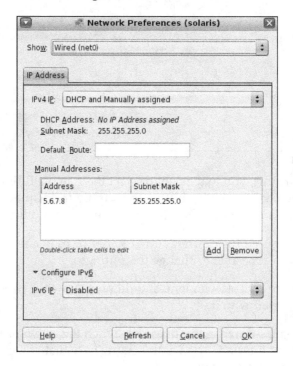

Locations

To recap, Locations are the containers for name services, IP security, and auto-configuration rules.

To view or edit locations, select the top-most item of the main window's pull-down menu, named **Connection Status**. It should then look somewhat like the following screenshot:

The location editing dialog is only accessible from this subarea.

Go ahead and click on the **Locations** button on the middle-right corner of the window. This will give you a new, separate dialog window named **Network Locations (solaris)**.

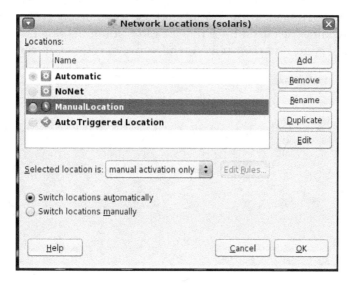

There are some predefined locations as shown in the previous screenshot: **Automatic** and **NoNet**. It's probably best to not edit these locations but choose one of them as your base and then duplicate it, if that is appropriate for your purpose.

Normally, a location entry can be activated either manually or by rules. If you choose the latter, the **Edit Rules** button becomes active, and you may click on it to pull up an additional dialog.

This dialog will allow you to specify settings, such as "activate this Location if Profile X is set", or "activate this Location if we have an IP address in range w.x.y.z".

For a location to be triggered by a Profile, you should first have created a profile. There is no "create a profile now" option.

If you wish to change locations manually, rather than writing rulesets, you will need to select the **Switch locations manually** radio button in the **Network Locations (solaris)** dialog.

 Each activation type confers a different icon to the location associated with it in the locations display.

When creating a new location, note that you cannot go back and rename a location after you first create it—the rename button lies. Effectively speaking, it is merely a **Duplicate** button, with an additional reminder for you to go back to delete the old one after you are done. Oddly, you cannot use **Rename** on the currently active one either. To rename the currently active location, you must first duplicate it with a more appealing name and then activate the *new* one, before you can remove the original one.

Summary

While most of this book is for Solaris sysadmins, and these days Oracle doesn't even officially sell a Solaris desktop any more, for those die-hard folks who like to run Solaris everywhere, it can make a pretty good laptop OS. Even wireless support is virtually painless if you run the official desktop and tools. NWAM is an additional tool that rounds out the networking making it easy to use for an average user.

The direct desktop integration of NWAM makes Solaris 11 comparable, or perhaps even superior, to many other common desktop OSs that support mobile networking.

Most people who use NWAM will probably use the GUI tool, which is why this chapter focuses on that interface. However, it should be noted that everything that can be done through the GUI can also be done through the command-line tools `netadm` and `netcfg`. Please consult the relevant Oracle documentation for those tools, if required.

6
ZFS – Now You Can't Ignore It!

This chapter covers the new features of the ZFS filesystem in Solaris 11.

Major ZFS topics covered in this chapter include:

- ZFS root — the new standard
- Boot time ZFS options
- Boot Environments and safe patching
- Deduplication, diffs, and encryption
- ZFS ACLs

ZFS – your future, today

Those people who are cautious about migrating to Solaris 11 may be equally as cautious about upgrading (or even using) the ZFS version already available to them on their production systems, and so might be unaware of the pending goodies that await them.

Having been in this category myself for sometime, I know how the routine goes — glance over the new stuff once to know what other people are talking about, but then ignore it. For this reason, even though some of the functionality mentioned in this chapter is not strictly *new to Solaris 11*, it will be covered here.

If some of the features here intrigue current Solaris 10 users, it is nice to know that most of them are available in Solaris 10 by fully patching it to MU10. The amount of hassle required to get there, however is almost equivalent to doing a full OS upgrade, so you may want to just plan a full upgrade anyway.

It is also important to realize that just applying patches does not in itself always give you new ZFS functionality. Usually, it is required that one run `zpool upgrade` and `zfs upgrade` to take advantage of the new features.

The good news is that those *upgrade* operations are non-destructive.

The bad news is that they can tie up the involved filesystems for quite a long time.

 Conversion time for a ZFS version upgrade of filesystems that have many files on them may take somewhere around 1 minute for every 1 to 5 GB of data that you have on it. During this time, you may find your filesystem to be write locked, which definitely has an impact on production systems. There are usually no issues, unless the filesystems or pools involved are more than 80% full.

Given this unfortunate detail, and the fact that you need downtime to patch and reboot for MU10, your best plan may be to plan upgrading any Solaris 10 system to Solaris 11. For one thing, it will make your future patching much safer, as mentioned later in the chapter.

ZFS root – no more UFS

One thing that may prove to be an emotional barrier to upgrading is that having your root filesystem on plain old UFS-on-disk-slices, mirrored or otherwise, is no longer an option. You *must* use ZFS as your root filesystem. The UFS filesystem is no longer supported as a bootable filesystem for Solaris 11.

 An apparent oddity for those who are familiar with ZFS best-practices is that ZFS root pools must be made on *disk slices* (format entities) rather than be set to use the entire disk. Normally, this would mean that ZFS would not fully optimize write-cache use. However, for root-disk pools, ZFS makes an exception and treats them in the same way that it treats ZFS-on-whole-disk pools.

Primary benefit of ZFS root filesystem

The ostensible reason for this forced change of root filesystem type is for mandatory patching safety. IPS, the new packaging and patching system, is integrated with ZFS. It insists on making a special bootable snapshot of a currently working system, before applying patches that have a high risk level to them.

Paranoid sysadmins may already be doing things such as splitting root mirrors off before patching, for "really important" system patching. Doing this the old way with DiskSuite has a few disadvantages as follows:

- Resync can take a relatively long time
- Booting to the other side and recovering properly, can be a major hassle

Even if you used **Live Upgrade**, and perhaps even borrowed a spare disk, you'd still have to fuss around with configuring slices and so on.

In contrast, the new ZFS snapshot method has some significant advantages to it:

- The system always stays mirrored.
- You can keep both OS versions around for a while and quickly alternate booting from either, with no hassle.
- No resync required on finish. Just delete the old snapshot when you are happy.

ZFS booting and beadm

Some folks may have already used Solaris Live Upgrade, to create separate instances of a root filesystem, primarily in order to safely patch systems and have targets for quick reboot or backup boot. Commands such as `lucreate` and `luactivate` will be familiar in the administration of these **Boot Environments** (**BEs**).

For those who like the `lu---` toolset, the good news is that the new replacement, `beadm` (Boot Environment Administrator) is functionally almost identical. You create, activate, and destroy Boot Environments in a similar way to before, but now Solaris 11 administrators now have a newly named unifying tool. The tool is designed, with relevant subcommands, in the new common style of a single frontend. Instead of using `lucreate xyz` and `luactivate xyz`, one uses `beadm create xyz` and `beadm activate xyz`.

Even better news is that the ZFS + IPS integration eliminates the necessity of by-hand steps for patching, including the rather tedious tasks of hunting down spare disk partitions for new BEs. So long as you have sufficient space in your root ZFS pool, `beadm` will take care of things by simply creating new filesystem(s) to shadow the normal required root disk type filesystems.

The patching/upgrade cycle has been improved even further. Rather than having to create a new Boot Environment by hand — first manually specifying your OS filesystems and then telling the patching commands to *go patch <over there>* — you now have one-stop shopping, albeit in slightly reverse order. Just give the IPS `pkg` command the switch to make a backup Boot Environment of your existing working OS when installing the updated versions of packages, and it will take care of all the details for you. In fact, when an IPS update involves significant change to the kernel, it will force creation of a saved Boot Environment rather than the old automatic patching backup style of copying old files under `/var/sadm/patch/SUNWxyz/save`. This is far superior in that you can have confidence that any particular BE will have a coherent and consistent set of packages installed rather than wondering which packages you may or may not have to back out piecemeal.

For those who hate the `lu---` set of commands, there is good news for you too!

One of the reasons you may have hated it is because it being a layered add-on, it was a little brittle when it came to making system changes. You had to use `init 6` after making Live Upgrade-type changes, or "bad things happened". This was because its boot time reconfiguration was, for some odd reason, done through startup/shutdown boot scripts.

With direct ZFS integration, the `beadm` command is a bit more robust. ZFS now has boot filesystem information integrated into the pool information. There is a pool property named `bootfs`, which obviously specifies which ZFS filesystem in the pool is the current root filesystem. It is still best practice to use `init 6`, but there are no longer dire warnings about forgetting to use it.

New boot-time options

There are new ZFS-root related options for boot time, which do not exist for UFS-based root systems.

While Solaris x86 and Solaris SPARC are almost identical at the running OS level, they are still extremely different at low-level boot time, so the options are covered separately for each architecture.

New SPARC boot options

- `boot -L`: Lists available environments
- `boot -Z rpoot/ROOT/somenamehere`: Boot from specific known environment

The `boot -L` option should list the descriptive name given for each BE and prompt you for your choice. It will then tell you what arguments to use with `boot -Z` to actually boot into it if you wish. In some ways, it is like a two-step GRUB menu.

Interestingly, it would appear to be actually implemented in partial GRUB fashion. The output comes from a plain-text file, `rpool/boot/menu.1st`.

Unfortunately, this would appear to be an auto-generated, non-authorative file. If you get the bright idea to hand-edit it, your changes will show up with `boot -L`, but not in `beadm list`, and it will most likely be overwritten by the next beadm change you make.

New x86 boot options

- `boot -B`: Boot from specific ZFS filesystem in rpool

It is common for the x86 GRUB menu to already have multiple choices for boot, easily selected by arrow key or number. `beadm` usually takes care of setting these up for you. However, if perhaps you have done things manually, it is good to know that you can edit or copy an existing GRUB `menu.1st` entry live (with the *E* key) to adjust the `-B` setting and then boot into your desired alternative root filesystem.

ZFS root limitations

All boot environments with `beadm`, are created in the root pool. This has advantages and disadvantages.

The biggest advantage is that you no longer have to think about allocation of disk space before setting up a new Boot Environment.

The biggest disadvantage is that you're not allowed to think about allocation of disk space before setting up a new Boot Environment.

Note that all OS-related filesystems, except for `/var`, must live under the *root* filesystem.

Also note that Oracle recommends 4 to 6 GB of space per BE. So now you can tell your boss you are doing something useful with all the unused space on your root disks.

ZFS, beadm, and zones

It should be noted that there is no longer any such thing as a "sparse" zone. Each zone has its own ZFS root filesystem, and a ZFS tree under that. They no longer share the root filesystem of the global zone, although they may have a **clone** of the global root filesystem. This is similar to, yet different from, the old style of sharing the /usr filesystem as read-only. The similarity resides in the fact that, if no changes are made, you only take up one zone's worth of filesystem space. The differences are rather critical however; changes made in the original are not reflected in any clones. Furthermore, the clones are writable, rather than read-only by default. However, it is possible to set a zone to have an "immutable" root. See *Chapter 8, Security Improvements,* for more details.

The zone-specific root filesystem is usually contained under:

`$(zonepath)/rpool/ROOT`

Because of this, it is also possible (and in a way, mandatory) to run beadm for zones. More details on this are given in *Chapter 7, Zones in Solaris 11.*

Deduplication now possible

ZFS now offers the option of enabling deduplication. If you enable the dedup property of a filesystem, any newly written data blocks that are duplicates of others will be stored merely as a reference to the already existing block, sort of like a hard link for an identical file.

Do keep in mind that it is on a block-by-block level though, rather than some kind of gzip compression.

Execute the following:

```
(cat large1 large2 )> file1
(cat large1; echo "a"; cat large2) >file2
```

If you do so, the end of the file will not get the benefit of dedup, since the block data will be out of alignment. The first parts of the file might be deduplicated for however long the data in large1 fits into whole block sizes.

It is important to know that, while this is a filesystem-by-filesystem option, the deduplication happens at the pool level.

By default, deduplication happens via checksum match (the default checksum being SHA1). However, it is also possible to change the ZFS `checksum` property for dedup-enabled filesystems to be `verify`. In this case, an additional byte-for-byte comparison will be done if checksums on two blocks match before deduplication is used for that specific block of data.

Additional gotchas of `dedup` are as follows:

- When `dedup` is enabled, `df` and `zfs list` lie about your disk space.

  A trustworthy count of "real" space on disk only shows up via `zpool list` if `dedup` is enabled anywhere in the pool. In contrast, if you added up all the *used* space from `df` on each `fs` in a pool and the output of `zfs list -r pool`, the total would add up to more than the on-disk space really used by the pool. You may well get a number larger than the size of the entire pool.

- It can take up significant amounts of RAM.

  `http://hub.opensolaris.org/bin/view/Community+Group+zfs/dedup` is the official reference for this sort of thing and gives you lots of other information, such as how to estimate the gains of turning on ZFS deduplication. It is, however, a bit long. The super-short summary is that ZFS dedup requires *320 bytes of memory per ZFS block*. However, since ZFS block size is variable, there isn't a hard-and-fast rule. Different people estimate requirements differently. You may need anywhere between 640 MB and 2 GB of free RAM, per unique TB of data, to hold the ZFS dedup table in memory.

  If you do not have enough RAM to do this, you should not be enabling dedupliation.

- Deleting snapshots can take much, much longer for filesystems that have `dedup` enabled. For highly populated filesystems, it may take hours.

- It may adversely affect write performance in other ways. Consider that every block written needs to be checked against the dedup table.

In summary, dedup is a great feature for filesystems with fewer performance requirements, such as an archive filesystem or possibly home directories. Using it in high-performance filesystems, such as for database use, would be a bad idea.

ZFS encryption

On-disk encryption of a ZFS filesystem is now possible in Solaris 11 as well as with the latest patch levels of Solaris 10. There is a fair amount of flexibility in the forms available. Key length can be 128-, 192-, or 256-bit AES which, similar to a PGP key is not directly editable. Instead, the admin controls access by use of a passphrase, which is referred to as a **wrapping key**. The key can be in the following forms:

- Entered manually
- Kept in plain-text form in a file
- Kept in raw form in a file (even an automounted USB stick)
- PKCS local Solaris keystore (can also leverage hardware crypto devices this way)
- PKCS remote keystore (accessed via HTTPS)

The first form of directly inputting a key is the easiest to set up but is the most annoying to use on a true production system. The removable media option is good if your organization is big on the physical key style of security.

Keeping the key in a separate file can be more useful than it sounds, if you use zones. It is possible to configure a zone so that its key file is kept by the global zone. In this way, no process running within the zone itself ever has access to the decryption information.

A remote PKCS keystore has the benefit of being available automatically at boot time yet still never having to give the key out to anyone other than the keystore admins. The remote keystore itself can be an official **Oracle Key Manager** installation, which can verify access by means of PKCS certificates.

Before starting down the path of encrypting filesystems, it is important to keep in mind that the encryption acts similarly to how ZFS deduplication or compression work. The latest settings only take effect on data written after the setting was changed. Old data will keep the old state. This has two ramifications:

- While it is possible to turn on encryption on an existing filesystem, only new data will be encrypted.
- While it is possible to change the encryption key of a pre-configured encrypted ZFS filesystem, the older data will remain encrypted with the older key. This apparently is done in a way that is compliant with the **NIST SP800-57 key lifetime** standard.

It is also important to note that once on-disk encryption is enabled, you cannot turn it off for that filesystem.

Some examples of initiating ZFS encryption are as follows:

```
// Simple manual passphrase
# zfs create -o encryption=on zdata/secure
Enter passphrase for 'zdata/secure':
Enter again:


// Using pre-existing files with plaintext passphrase or raw data
# zfs create -o encryption=on -o keysource=passphrase=raw,\file:///media/
stick/pass zdata/secure
# zfs create -o encryption=on -o keysource=raw,file:///media/stick/rawkey
zdata/secure


// Use locally generated pkcs-format keys with native Solaris 11
 tools
// (presumes pre-existing knowledge of the Solaris keystore tools and
// pre-existing keystore)
# pktool genkey keystore=pkcs11 keytype=aes keylen=256 label=zfskey
Enter PIN for Sun Software PKCS#11 softtoken:
# zfs create -o encryption=on -o keysource=raw,pkcs11:object=zfskey
zdata/secure
Enter PKCS#11 token PIN for 'zdata/secure':


// Get the key from a remote, trusted SSL server
# cp servercert.pem /etc/certs/CA
# svcadm refresh ca-certificates
# zfs create -o encryption=on -o keysource=raw,https://server/zfs_key
zdata/secure
```

ZFS diff between snapshots

If you have one or more snapshots of a filesystem, you can now take advantage of the saved metadata to do fast difference checks between them, or with the current filesystem, rather than having to manually traverse the filesystem with `diff -r` or `rsync`. It's not always two-second fast, but it is certainly convenient when you already have a snapshot made.

The only downside is that it does not tell you the actual file content that has changed, only that the file has changed overall. Even so, I have found this to be quite useful on occasions. For example, if there is some install command that you are not 100 percent confident of in what it does, creating a pre-install snapshot and then a diff, can tell you with certainty what happened on even a very large filesystem, with minimal system impact.

It can also tell you which files have merely been renamed whereas a normal diff would tell you "*oldname* file has been removed: *newname* file has been created".

Technically, there are two forms to the `zfs diff` operation; compare snapshot to another snapshot or compare to its parent filesystem. For some reason, comparing snapshot to snapshot requires that you mount both snapshots, which makes it inconvenient to use, so I shall skip it here. The simpler form does not require anything other than the name of a snapshot. For example:

`zfs diff rpool/export/archives@weeklysnapshot`

This will mention to you the name of every file that has been modified, renamed, or deleted since the referenced snapshot.

In the following example, an initial snapshot was created, and then the obvious operations took place on files with the relevant names. It is interesting to see that in addition to the regular files, the directory containing the deleted file is also marked as modified, as the directory "file" has indeed been changed.

```
# rm deleted_file
# mv renamed_file newname_file
# echo morestuff >>modified_file
# zfs snapshot rpool/export@snap2
# zfs diff  rpool/export@snap1  rpool/export@snap2
M    /export/
M    /export/modified_file
R    /export/renamed_file → /export/newname_file
-    /export/deleted_file
```

ZFS's new ACL modes – simpler yet more powerful

ZFS introduces a new style of Access Control List (ACL) as compared to Solaris UFS ACLs. Previously, ACLs were based around POSIX-style ACL specs. The new model is closer to Windows NT-style ACLs and NFSv4 standards.

The reason for this change is to allow a more granular set of privileges and more options for inheritance in subdirectories.

The older style of ACL is no longer supported on ZFS. If you attempt to use setfacl or getfacl on new ZFS, it will give you an error similar to the following one:

```
File system doesn't support aclent_t style ACL's
```

To separate use of this new style from the older model, examination and changes to new style ACLs are done with ls and chmod. Happily, it is much simpler for common operations.

Viewing ACLs on a file

As previously mentioned, you will know that there are ACLs set on a file if there is a + at the end of the permissions column of ls -l output. However, the methods for viewing the details as well as the output are different from those previously mentioned. There is also a long form and a short form of viewing ACLs. Each ACL permission type has its own single-letter abbreviation, sort of like how chmod 0400 can also be called chmod u+rw.

Use ls -V to see the abbreviated form and ls -v to see the fully expanded and numbered form.

In the following example, some strange person has decided to allow user mysql to have write permission to the zshrc file:

```
# ls -l zshrc
-r-r--r--+  1 root        bin      177  Oct 20  2011 zshrc
# ls -V zshrc
-r-r--r--+  1 root        bin      177  Oct 20  2011 zshrc
            user:mysql:-w------------:-------:allow
              owner@:r-----aARWcCos:-------:allow
              group@:r-----a-R-c--s:-------:allow
           everyone@:r-----a-R-c--s:-------:allow
# ls -v zshrc
```

```
0:user:mysql:write_data:allow
```

```
1:owner@:read_data/read_xattr/write_xattr/read_attributes
    /write_attributes/read_acl/write_acl/write_owner/synchronize:allow
```

```
2:group@:read_data/read_xattr/read_attributes/read_acl/synchronize:al
low
```

```
3:everyone@:read_data/read_xattr/read_attributes/read_acl/synchronize
:allow
```

It is important to note two things about this output:

- The default permissions in the "mode 0444" style are integrated with the ACL listing, with the special line designations of owner@, group@, and everyone@. This becomes very important when comes the time to set an ACL or even to use chmod in regular fashion, so make sure to read the *Setting an ACL* section thoroughly as well.

- There are some permission styles that you probably don't recognize, such as, read_xattr.

Setting an ACL

For a simple example to allow user mysql to write to /etc/zshrc, you can use either of the following forms:

- chmod A+user:mysql:write_data:allow /etc/zshrc

- chmod A+user:mysql:w:allow /etc/zshrc

This will add an ACL to the file, allowing the desired permissions.

 Using a standard chmod syntax after this point, such as chmod 0444 /etc/zshrc, will *clear* any non-standard ACLs set on the file.

As hinted in the *Viewing ACLs on a file* section, permissions of the standard chmod style are more or less just another set of ACLs. The longer form of the old, tried-and-tested chmod 0644 file style command is as follows:

chmod A=owner@:rw:allow,group@:r:allow,everyone@:r:allow file

Note the use of A= rather than A+. This means "override all existing ACLs and set permissions to be exactly what is on this line".

As they are literally synonymous, doing `chmod 0644 file` will also override all existing ACLs. This is different from Solaris UFS, where `chmod` operations did not alter `setfacl` operations.

Sometimes, you will want to replace—or simply delete—an ACL on a file. There are simple one-line equivalents to do each of these things. To do item-by-item modifications, you should first use `ls -v` to get an indexed listing of the ACLs, as demonstrated in the prior section of this chapter. Then, to modify or delete the ACL line labeled `0`, use the following command:

```
chmod A0=user:mysql:rw:allow zshrc

// Changed my mind, just nuke it

chmod A0- zshrc
```

There is even a one-line shortcut for "remove all non-standard ACLs".

```
// Ah, the heck with it, I just want to make sure it's all "normal"
// terms again now

chmod A- zshrc
```

For a full list of the short and long forms to use with the new ACLs, see *Appendix B, New ACL Permissions and Abbreviations*.

Miscellaneous changes and improvements

- The default output of `zfs list` is to *not* list snapshots. To see them, you must either add `-t snapshot` or `-t all`. Using `-r` will not display them either.

- The speed of doing deep directory searches has reportedly been improved significantly.

- Now in addition to raidz2, you have an alternative of raidz3 as well. Yes, three disk parity sets.

Pool-related changes

- There is now a read-only pool `import` option.

  Sometimes, when an exported pool has been damaged or corrupted, it may still be possible to import it to recover data, using the following command:

  ```
  zpool import -o readonly=on poolname
  ```

- If you have created a pool with a separate log device (IE on an SSD), the pool would not be importable if the device failed. In Solaris 11, it is now possible to force import with `-m`.

- If you have forgotten the name of a pool that you need, but you are sure of one of the device paths in the pool, you can use the `-d` option, thus:

  ```
  zpool import -d /dev/dsk/c5t4d3 [optional-poolname-override]
  ```

- If a zpool is mirrored, you may now use `zpool split` to split it into two separate pools. This is useful for sending a set of disks offsite, or just to a system in another rack.

- It is now possible to assign quotas to a user; however, unlike UFS quotas, the ZFS per-user quota is system-wide.

Summary

ZFS in Solaris 11 has had some powerful enhancements added to what was already a first-class enterprise filesystem. Multiple NAS vendors are now basing their offerings around ZFS.

On top of an amazingly robust filesystem, the serviceability integration given to OS upgrades and patching make it an outstanding base for the Solaris OS to run on. Even if you do not plan on making use of all the available features right away, it's almost a certainty that you will have an opportunity to use many of them in the future.

> **Crucial Tip for adding features to an existing/older ZFS pool**
>
> If you are importing a ZFS pool from an older version of Solaris, you may not be able to use the newer features right away. Remember that you need to upgrade the ZFS pool and filesystem versions via `zpool upgrade`, and `zfs upgrade` respectively. Remember also that these operations are non-reversible, and that ZFS filesystem version upgrades can have an impact on production during the time period the upgrade is taking place.

7
Zones in Solaris 11

Solaris 11 zones have some significant differences from Solaris 10 zones. Some features are no longer there, but others have replaced them. Zones in Solaris 11 are a few steps closer to being completely independent virtual machines in their own right yet still retain the performance and interoperability advantages of zones.

Taking things to the next zone

Zones in Solaris 11 come with some new utilities, new features, and some mandatory differences in basic setup and usage. Key new features covered in this chapter are:

- zonestat
- New zone capabilities, including zone `beadm`
- anet, the new auto-configuring zone network interface type
- How to preconfigure zones
- Read-only zones, aka immutable zones

New zone utilities

The most useful new utility is `zonestat`. Similar in principle to the other `*stat` tools, it will give you a repeating snapshot over time of relevant resources being used, where you tell it the interval between each output. It was actually possible already to get per-zone statistics with `prstat -Z`, but that forced you to look at "ps" style output as well.

In contrast, the new zonestat tool has many more options, and its output is focused purely on entire zone-level usage. See the manpage for full details, but in general terms, zonestat lets you see each zone's total CPU, memory, and network bandwidth usage.

It is possible to run the zonestat command within a zone, but you will only see statistics for that zone.

An additional tool of interest is zonep2vchk. The purpose of this tool is to check for potential difficulties when transferring a **physical zone** (that is, a global zone) "**2**" a **virtual** one. Its default mode is to look at installed services to see if they are compatible with running in a zone. A counter-example to this is that it will detect that VirtualBox services, if running, are not compatible with zones.

To take things even further, use of zonep2vchk -s will do an in-depth scan of ELF binaries to attempt to detect non-portable binaries.

New zone capabilities

Solaris 11 zones have a few extra capabilities, some of which have been awaited for a long time now.

- Zones can now be NFS servers. There's not much more to be said about that, other than "it's about time!".

- zoneadm can now do shutdown and reboot, in addition to halt.

- Zones can now run snoop successfully, and safely, if the zone has its own private network interface. While it was technically possible to allow snoop in a zone under Solaris 10, it was necessary to take some dubious and unsafe shortcuts to do so.

Thanks to the drastic rewriting of how the Solaris 11 kernel handles networking, this does not mean that the zone needs its own dedicated physical network interface. It is possible to allocate a virtual NIC (VNIC) device to a zone, and safely allow the zone to use snoop, without letting it see traffic from other zones that may share the same physical interface.

- It is also possible to allow a zone to manage its own IP address. It is even possible for a zone to use DHCP, if the zone is given its own Ethernet address (which can be done automatically).

- Zones now always have their own ZFS-based, independent root filesystems. By default, they have the zoned property set on them. This also gives them, by default, the following abilities:

  ° The ability to make their own snapshots.

  ° The ability to make and manage their own Boot Environments (BEs) through beadm.

  ° The ability to manage their own packages. Technically, this isn't new, but it has a new mandatory style since the old default was to have zones inherit packages from the global zone.

Changes to zones

Along with the new features, there are some things in Solaris 11 zones that are just plain *different*.

Allowable zone OS types limited

In Solaris 10, in addition to the default Solaris 10 zones, you could have zones running Solaris 8 and 9 or even some versions of Linux.

In Solaris 11, you can now unfortunately only have Solaris 10 zones (and, of course, Solaris 11 zones).

ZFS zoneroot layout and Boot Environments

The ZFS filesystem layout of a zone is now designed to look pretty much identical to a top-level global zone.

A sample auto-created tree of OS-related filesystems for testzone should look like the following:

/zones/testzone

/zones/testzone/rpool

/zones/testzone/rpool/ROOT

/zones/testzone/rpool/ROOT/solaris

/zones/testzone/rpool/ROOT/solaris/var

As you can see, if you replace `/zones/testzone/` with `/`, it is the same layout you see in your global zone under `/rpool`. This makes zone management almost identical to global zone management. This is not merely to make things look consistent.

Zones now have their own Boot Environments, independent from the global zone!

This means that, yes, you use `beadm` in zones to manage a zone's Boot Environment separately from the global zone. Thus, you can create snapshots of a particular Boot Environment or package configuration within a zone in the same way that you can do so for a global zone. You can also quickly toggle between which configuration will be active at next zone reboot, with `beadm activate`.

The different BEs for a zone, are completely separate from, and invisible to, the BEs for the machine's global zone.

Fast zone creation via clone

In Solaris 10, you may or may not have been taking advantage of zones on ZFS, and thus, zone cloning.

In Solaris 11, since you *must* give each zone its own ZFS subfilesystem, you may as well take advantage of cloning if you plan on creating more than one zone. This is particularly relevant given that, by default, all zones are created with the same small set of packages, but it can still take quite a while to initialize. In contrast, when using `zoneadm -z newzone clone oldzone`, installing a new zone takes only 10 to 15 seconds.

> The one drawback of using the `zoneadm` clone is that you cannot clone a currently running zone. However, if you plan ahead and create your first running zone from a non-running template zone, you will take up no extra disk space and will also have a template immediately available for your next zone.

If you use cloning to create a zone, the new ZFS root filesystem will initially be a writable ZFS clone of the old zone filesystem, presuming you have them in the same ZFS pool (which you should!). This gives you perfect initial *data deduplication* even if you choose not to enable deduplication on the filesystem(s) for performance reasons. Do note, however, that disk space for any future package additions or updates will not be shared across zones unless you do turn on actual deduplication in ZFS.

Because of the clone capabilities, it makes a lot of sense to have a top-level /zones pool or filesystem and standardize on zonecfg zonepath values always being /zones/ZONENAME. This is true even if some zones require their own pools or unique filesystems for performance reasons. The good thing about ZFS is that creating subfilesystems is comparatively cheap.

The zoned property of ZFS

The zoned property of ZFS is not strictly new but is worthwhile repeating here.

Zones will automatically get a *root* filesystem created for them, with the zoned ZFS property. At present, zone creation will fail if you provide a manually created filesystem for it that does not have the property set.

Having the zoned property set, is important for normal zone operation as well as package management and use of beadm requires the creation of snapshots and new filesystems. It is so important in fact, that upon zone boot the property will automatically be restored, if you accidentally decided to turn it off.

If you do not wish to grant this level of flexibility to zones, see the *Immutable zones* section of this chapter.

Zone filesystems visible

It used to be that, if filesystems were delegated to a zone (by defining a ZFS dataset in zonecfg), the global zone could not always see them and all filesystems would be unmounted when the zone was not running.

In Solaris 11, the OS-related ZFS filesystems for a zone remain mounted and visible for the global zone, even after the child zone has been halted. Other filesystems, such as /export/home, do not show up in df but do show up with mount -p.

Automatic Network Interfaces – the anet resource

The old **net** resource for zones has been somewhat deprecated, in favor of a new name, anet. Technically, it stands for **Automated Network Interface**, but it also adds a few new capabilities that could have been added to the regular net resource but were not.

Zones now, by default, have a network type of **exclusive** rather than **shared**. This may be a little misleading to Solaris 10 admins since that previously implied an entire physical network interface would be dedicated to the zone. Happily, this is no longer required.

Solaris 11 zones make use of the new **Virtual Network Interface**, aka **VNIC**. It is now standard procedure for a zone to have its own VNIC, which is in some ways similar to the concept of a virtual interface under VMware or VirtualBox. The VNIC device usually has its own automatically generated Ethernet address and so can be a fully functional direct member of your network, including the use of DHCP, VLAN tagging, and anything else a *real* network interface can do.

To facilitate this style of configuration, the `anet` resource has two properties of principal interest: the `linkname` property, which determines the name the zone will see for its device, and the `lower-link` property, which determines which global-zone level device will actually be used.

The truncated output of `zonecfg -z xyz info anet` will typically look like this:

```
anet:
    linkname: net0
    lower-link: auto
```

Using the `auto` value allows the system to randomly choose which physical device to create a VNIC on top of. However, you can also specify one manually.

From the global zone, these anet-allocated devices do not show up in the output of `ifconfig -a` or even `ipadm show-addr`. You can see VNICs in use by zones only by the use of either `dladm show-vnic` or `dladm show-link`.

To prevent abuse by delegated zone-root privileges, the `anet` resource also makes many limiters available for sysadmin use. You can preconfigure a VLAN ID, a MAC address, and/or an *allowed* range of IP addresses the zone may use. It also has default anti-spoofing protection for the Ethernet address, via:

```
link-protection: mac-nospoof
```

It is this setting that makes it safe to give zone-root authority to use snoop and similar low-level networking tools since the zone will only be able to use its own MAC address and will only be able to see traffic appropriate for its own MAC address. Other values for this property come from whatever is permissible by the dladm *protection* feature. See *dladm(1M)* for more details.

A zone, by default, can now change its own IP address unless you set the `allowed-address` property on the anet resource.

Preconfiguring zones

Zone configuration has three basic levels to it, which can be automated at one or all levels.

Sysconfig information

In Solaris 10 zones, it was possible to preconfigure sys-unconfig type information, (hostname, name service, and so on) by prepopulating /etc/sysidcfg before first boot. In Solaris 11, there is a similar concept, but with a very different implementation. First of all, as the relevant file is now XML-based, you are best off using the `sysconfig create-profile` subcommand to generate it for you. Secondly, you are now expected to pass the location of the file as an argument to `zoneadm install`. The following examples will hopefully make this clearer:

- `zoneadm -z newzone install -c /path/to/sysconfig.xml`

- `zoneadm -z newzone clone -c /path/to/sysconfig.xml oldzone`

The two crucial things here are that you must give the full path to the XML file, and that if you are cloning, you must give the old zone name last on the command line.

Initial zonecfg defaults

There is only one mandatory setting that must be specified through `zonecfg` when creating a new zone: zonepath. All other values that can be set by `zonecfg` are set from a special template file for zones.

The default `zonecfg` template is /etc/zones/SYSdefault.xml. This happens to be the same directory where regular zone configuration information is stored, so be careful in there.

If you would like to create a different template, it is best to copy the existing one to a new one rather than to edit it.

To make use of your new template in `zonecfg`, use `create -t` as follows:

```
#cp /etc/zones/SYSdefault.xml /etc/zones/MYzonecfg.xml
// (edit MYzonecfg.xml)
# zonecfg -z newzone 'create -t MYzonecfg ; \
set zonepath=/zones/newzone'
```

To make your new template the default one, you must change the zone-related SMF property, as follows:

```
svccfg -s zones setprop zonecfg/default_template = MYzonecfg
```

(The full SMF path is `svc:/system/zones:default`.)

It is still possible to use `zonecfg ... -f commandfile` to create a new zone, with or without a new custom template. The advantage of using a template is that templates are allowed to have partially complete information. For example, the zone name and the zone path would not be expected to be in a zone template. In contrast, when you invoke `zonecfg` with the `-f` option, you are expected to deliver the full set of required information for a zone.

Initial package content of zones

In Solaris 10, unless a zone was cloned from an existing one via `zoneadm`, it received a copy of all packages installed on the global zone. For Solaris 11 however, the initial contents are determined quite differently.

A new Solaris 11 zone does not take its package contents from what packages are installed on the global zone. Nor does it get updated when you add or remove packages from the global zone.

By default, the filesystems locally controlled by a zone and the package contents of a new zone are determined by:

```
/usr/share/auto_install/manifest/zone_default.xml
```

This manifest is read by `zoneadm` at the time that you run `zoneadm install`.

The Oracle default zone directives consist primarily of ensuring that an `/export/home` filesystem be created and that the package set installed for a new zone is the collection known as `pkg:/group/system/solaris-small-server`.

This is a considerably small set of packages (only 171 at the current time) and has the benefit of making new zone creation faster but is probably smaller than you would otherwise like.

It has the additional benefit that it is the exact same default package set that a new Solaris 11 install will deliver on fresh hardware.

To have a different set of packages installed at zone installation time, you must specify an entire manifest to override the default one at zone install time. One example of doing this is as follows:

```
cd /usr/share/auto_install/manifest
sed 's:solaris-small-server:solaris-large-server:' zone_default.xml >
large-server.xml
zoneadm -z newzone install -m large-server.xml
```

The `zone_default.xml` manifest file is quite lengthy, so we will not go into full details about it in this book.

Example of fully preconfigured zone creation

Putting together some of the concepts previously mentioned, here is an example of almost completely hands-off zone creation, if you have gone to the trouble of making your own `zonecfg` template, xxx template, and the `sysconfig` generated profile `sysprofile.xml` (aka a SC profile):

```
zonecfg -z newzone 'create -t MYzonecfg ; /
set zonepath=/zones/newzone'
zoneadm -z newzone install -m
/usr/share/auto_install/manifest/zone_large.xml -c \
  /path/to/sysprofile.xml
```

This will be ready to run as soon as you boot it up, but it will take a long time. It will still have to run first boot SMF configuration but should not prompt you for basic information such as hostname and network information.

Unfortunately, there may be some bugs where `sysprofile` does not fully configure the new zone, and you may need `sysconfig unconfigure` to set things up manually. Caveat emptor!

Alternatively, you can use this in conjunction with zone cloning to speed up creation time.

```
zoneadm -z newzone clone -c /path/to/sysprofile.xml oldzone
```

Order matters. `oldzone` must come last on the line, or you will get error messages similar to "no such zone configured".

Don't be alarmed when a preconfigured zone outputs a line on its console, `Hostname: unknown`. Give it a bit more time, and it should reconfigure itself appropriately.

Immutable zones

In Solaris 10, it was common to have zones created with read-only versions of `/usr`, shared from the global zone. This had assorted benefits, one of which was to disallow overwriting of system binaries from the zone.

Solaris 11 zones offer the option of having fixed, or **immutable** zones. The typical configuration will lock down *all* files other than those under clearly volatile filesystems such as `/tmp` and `/var/tmp` (including local filesystems such as `/export/home`).

It is possible to choose from three different types of immutable configurations. They have varying degrees of inhibition, but all of them have the following features in common:

- It is no longer possible to install IPS packages
- Persistently enabled SMF services cannot be changed
- SMF manifests cannot be added from the normal locations

The three individualized types of immutable zones, set through the `file-mac-profile` property of `zonecfg` are as follows:

- `flexible-configuration`: This is similar to the prior **sparse-zone** configuration in that it effectively has a read-only `/usr` directory, but files in the root's home directory, and `/etc`, are usually adjustable. Unlike sparse zones however, SMF service configurations cannot be changed.

- `fixed-configuration`: This is a more restrictive setting, which in addition to the preceding limitations, disables changes to `/etc`. Most files in `/var` — other than system configuration — are still writable however.

- `strict`: This is the most restrictive setting. Every standard system path is read-only. Even logging and audit data updates are not allowed; output must be configured to be stored remotely.

It is still possible to make temporary changes to things such as SMF properties and services; however, these changes will be reverted upon next reboot.

Making a zone immutable is done at the `zonecfg` level. It is good to keep that in mind when doing such things as cloning zones, which is done at the `zoneadm` level. This is further explained in the next section.

Creating an immutable zone

Any zone can be turned into an immutable zone by using the following commands:

```
# zonecfg -z ZONENAME 'set file-mac-profile=fixed-configuration'
# zoneadm -z ZONENAME reboot #or reboot from inside zone
```

If a fully read-only zone is desired, disallowing even /var/tmp and /var/log, use a profile value of `strict` instead.

> The read-only settings of `file-mac-profile` do not apply to any additional ZFS pools or other filesystems manually added onto the zone configuration in `zonecfg`.

Verifying immutable zone configuration

To view the immutability status of multiple zones in a concise manner, append the -p option to `zoneadm list`, as follows. Note the final column of the output, which shows the `file-mac-profile` setting.

```
# zoneadm list -p
0:global:running:/::solaris:shared:-:none
1:normalzone:running:/zones/normalzone:(UUID):solaris:excl:-:
2:securezone:running:/zones/securezone:(UUID):solaris:excl:R:strict
3:partialsecurezone:running:/zones/pzone:(UUID):solaris:excl:R:fixed-configuration
```

It is useful to know that, if a normally immutable zone has been temporarily mounted in read/write mode, the preceding listing would show `:W:` instead of the expected `:R:` in the second-to-last column.

Cloning an immutable zone

It is possible to clone an immutable zone, but there are some important things to keep in mind. Cloning does not copy the `fixed` attribute. That turns out to be a good thing since a zone needs to go through a "self-assembly" phase at first boot, and that requires write access to its filesystems.

There are two ways to handle this issue:

- The more "hands-on" approach.

```
// (zonecfg has already been done normally)
# zoneadm -z newzone clone srczonename
# zoneadm -z newzone boot
# zlogin -C newzone
// (Answer config questions)


# zonecfg -z newzone 'set file-mac-profile=fixed-
configuration'
# zoneadm -z newzone reboot
```

- The more automated approach. This works particularly well if you have first boot zone configuration automated.

  The key difference in this example is the uppercase -W option. This tells the zone to do boot-time things and to reboot afterwards in read-only mode.

```
// (zonecfg has already been done,
// with file-mac-profile=fixed-configuration)
# zoneadm -z newzone clone [-c optional_sysconfig_file.xml]\
srczonename
# zoneadm -z newzone boot -W
// This will automatically boot in read/write mode,
// do self-configuration, and the reboot immediately.
// If you do NOT have first-boot sysconfig information
// automated, you can still answer through
# zlogin -C newzone
```

Updating immutable zone configurations

If you need to make adjustments to an immutable zone, you will need two reboots, such as the following:

```
global# zoneadm -z ZONENAME (re)boot -w

zone# (make changes here)

zone# (reboot, and zone will then be read-only again)
```

It is important to note that you should use lowercase -w to enable manual changes to the zone. In contrast, for more automated changes, you may use uppercase version of -W, as shown in the *Cloning an immutable zone* section.

For security purposes, it is crucial to plan, schedule, and finish any manual changes to an immutable zone. While the writability window of using boot -w will only last until next reboot, you do have to remember to reboot again the second time!

To avoid the phenomenon of zones believed secure being left in a less secure state, it may be advisable to setup a monitoring on the top in the global zone, with zoneadm list -p (as mentioned earlier), to verify that an immutable zone is not left in a writeable state for too long.

Summary

Zones in Solaris 11 are even closer to the capabilities of a fully autonomous VM, yet with the performance efficiencies of a shared kernel. With the extremely fast creation and boot capabilities they provide, (not to mention the zero incremental license cost), there is very little reason to use a full-blown VM solution any more. In fact, even if you still need one, you can now use Oracle VM for free. Support for it costs extra but is based on physical number of CPU sockets rather than number of VMs.

With the added observability of zonestat, plus the greater autonomy of zone-local Boot Environments, you can now have a virtual datacenter on a single commodity priced box. This all comes without the barriers of inter-VM communication that full virtualization solutions tend to bring along with them as baggage.

8
Security Improvements

To avoid locking the barn door after the horse has bolted, it's good to be aware that there is a lock available for you to use in the first place. Take a moment to peruse the assortment of new locks available in Solaris 11.

Alongside some miscellaneous changes, the major deadbolts covered in this chapter are:

- Auditing changes
- Immutable zones
- Sudo
- Encrypted ZFS

Keeping the horse in the barn

There is an assortment of new security-related features in Solaris 11, in very disparate areas. I would recommend that you glance at all the items in this chapter. Even if you don't use them right away, they may prove useful to you at some point in the future.

Mandatory auditing

Auditing is now enabled by default in Solaris 11. Previously, enabling auditing required running the `bsmconv` tool, and then rebooting. Now, however, it is an SMF service, `svc://system/auditd:default`, and can be enabled and disabled without rebooting. Additional good news is that there have been some internal performance optimizations for auditing as well.

Audit changes now must be done only through `auditconfig`. It is no longer possible to edit the old plaintext file `/etc/security/audit_startup`.

As usual for the audit daemon, logs are stored by default in the `/var/audit` directory. It is possible for each zone to have its own audit logs, or for the global zone to be responsible for everything. See the *Audit policies* section of this chapter for more details.

Auditing basics

For those people who have not previously had to deal with auditing under Solaris, here is a brief overview. Audit logging allows you to record various events that happen to the system. Such events can include:

- Login attempts (both successful and unsuccessful)
- Process execution
- File access (open, create, write, and read)
- RBAC role usage

The ones mentioned here are the most common points of interest. However, practically every system call can be recorded, if desired. See `/etc/security/audit_event` for the full list of all initially known events. It is also possible to define custom event types.

Audit logs can grow very large and very fast on an active system, depending on what policies you set and which events you configure to log. You should therefore only enable logging of data that you are likely to actually use.

Default audit events

By default, Solaris 11 auditing will configure itself to only record high-level events, such as login events using `su` and `sudo` commands. It will record as much information as is known about what user, when, and from where the events took place. You can view which events are going to be currently recorded with the `-getflags` option. Expected default output is shown as follows:

```
# auditconfig -getflags
active user default audit flags = lo(0x1000,0x1000)
configured user default audit flags = lo(0x1000,0x1000)
```

The output says that the system is configured to record events of type lo. This is actually an audit class, rather than a single event. Events to be logged are always referred to via class rather than directly.

Audit classes are defined in /etc/security/audit_class. Looking up the value yields the following:

```
# grep :lo: /etc/security/audit_class
0x0000000000001000:lo:login or logout
```

Though in /etc/security/audit_event there are over 700 preconfigured audit events, there are only around 30 preconfigured audit classes. There is a catchall type class named all, but using this for any extended period is not advisable, due to the size of logfiles and potential system impact.

Configuring more audit logging

To add more audit events to be logged, first look at /etc/security/audit_class to determine which ones are of interest to you, and then add them either to the system-wide configs or to an individual user.

Let's say you wish to record all program executions, but in addition, you wish to record all file creation events by the user anonftp. You would normally do this as follows:

```
// First, check what the current flags are, so you don't lose any
// additions
# auditconfig -getflags


// Now add in the execution flag to the default "lo"
# auditconfig -setflags exec,lo


// And finally, adjust log levels for the anonftp user to include the
// previous, plus fc(filecreate) class
# usermod -K exec,lo,fc:no anonftp
```

Audit policies

There are some policies that can be set above and beyond what events to log.

To view a list of possible policies, use `auditconfig -lspolicy`. At present, there are 15 available, which include things such as:

- `arge`: Includes process environment in a log of an executed program.
- `argv`: Includes full arguments, rather than just process name, of an executed program.
- `zonename`: Includes the zone name in the records. Useful if the global zone logs for all zones.
- `perzone`: When set in the global zone, each zone becomes responsible for its own audit logs.

By default, Solaris 11 has only one audit related policy enabled: `cnt`.

Unlike most of the other policies, this is not related to log format but is a policy to keep the system running (that is, to "CoNTinue") when audit space runs out. If this is not set, the system could default to becoming nonfunctional if audit space runs out.

The following output shows what to expect to see with the default audit policies:

```
# auditconfig -getpolicy
configured audit policies = cnt
active audit policies = cnt
```

Active versus configured values

Some of the previous examples may point out the concept of active versus configured settings. Configured settings are values saved in the SMF internal database. It is possible to override the SMF settings by using a `-t` flag, similar to when temporarily adjusting IP or SMF service values. In those cases, you would see different outputs in the lines for active versus configured values.

Viewing audit logs

The logs are normally kept in a binary format to conserve space. To view the contents of a logfile, use the `praudit` command. You can use either multiline output (typically three lines at a time), which is the default, or single line output with the `-1` option (which is the same, but simply without the extra line feeds):

```
# praudit  /var/audit/YYYYMMDDhhmmss.YYYYMMDDhhmmss

file,2012-07-24 46.075 -07:00,

header,52,2,system booted,na,localhost,2012-07-24 09:46:12.501 -07:00
text,booting kernel header,42,2,init(1m),na,localhost,2012-07-24
09:48:31.734 -07:00

text,booted return,success,0
header,69,2,login - ssh,,localhost,2012-07-24 09:49:05.532 -07:00

subject,root,root,root,root,root,1202,765442113,2733 71168
somehost.company.com return,success,0
```

For a very detailed description of each field of output, see the *audit.log(4)* manpage.

Immutable zones

Full configuration details for immutable zones are covered in *Chapter 7, Zones in Solaris 11*, but it is worth mentioning the rationale for them here.

To have an almost hack-proof system, it is very effective to take away write access from it as much as possible. If you are willing to run your services in a zone, it is possible to configure that zone as an immutable zone. This allows you to render filesystems and even service configurations as *immutable* (that is, non-writable).

Most remote attacks succeed by eventually writing corrupted data to the filesystem, and then taking more control from there. If they cannot write to the filesystem, many avenues of attack are closed. Furthermore, if they cannot deface the site, or store their own files, the incentive for taking over the system may also have been removed.

There are varying levels of immutability possible. If your services will not run in a fully read-only zone, it is possible to allow access to `/var`, and a few other filesystems.

ProFTPd is the new FTP server

For a very long time, the FTP server bundled with Solaris has been based on the WU-FTPd program. In Solaris 11, this has been changed to ProFTPd.

In addition to being more current, easier to configure, and more flexible, ProFTPd has the advantage of being more secure. The ProFTPd team takes security very seriously; it has a mailing list, security@proftpd.org, dedicated to resolving any security issues in a timely manner.

The best practice for setting up anonymous FTP is to create a chroot directory. In older FTP daemons, this required setting up a special directory with copies of standard libraries. Some people may have avoided doing so due do this complexity.

ProFTPd eliminates this requirement, thus encouraging better security practices.

In addition to improvements for anonymous FTP, ProFTPd gives the ability to force all users to be "chrooted" on login. This means that FTP users will not be able to change the directory (cd) outside their home directory. This is done by setting the DefaultRoot directive in the configuration file appropriately.

The configuration file for ProFTPd is similar to the Apache syntax. This makes the context of directives important. Because of this, it is best to look at whole configuration files in full context, rather than single line snippets. For full details on its many other configuration options, see http://www.proftpd.org/docs/.

Sudo privileged access tool

The sudo tool (aka "su do") has long been a favorite of Unix admins (including MacOS), but prior to now, had to be installed from third parties on Solaris. Now in Solaris 11, it comes as part of the base OS package.

For those people who have somehow never used it before—don't worry, it's quite simple to use. The user interface is a little like Solaris pfexec. In the simplest case, you simply insert the word sudo in front of any command you wish to run with root privileges. For example:

```
sudo snoop
```

If you have not run the sudo command in the last few minutes, it will ask for your password (not the root password, but your own). It will then cache a successful entry so you do not have to enter your password every time.

It is also possible to run commands as other users quite easily. For example:

```
sudo -u apache apachectl restart
```

All this presupposes that there is an appropriate entry for your account in the sudoers config file.

Here are a collection of sample sudoers entries, going from simplest to more complex:

```
# {userspec} {allowedhosts} = {(runas_user)} {commandline}
operator ALL = /sbin/halt
superguy ALL = ALL
joe joesbox = /sbin/halt
webadmin web1,web1 = (apache) /usr/apache/bin/apachectl
Host_Alias INFOWEB = infoweb1,infoweb2,infoweb3
User_Alias WEBOPSGRP = joe, jack, jill
WEBOPS INFOWEB = (apache) /usr/apache/bin/apachectl restart
%admgrp +hostnetgrp = NOPASSWD: /fancy/admin/tool
```

Some important things to note are as follows:

- Each of the four main fields can use aliases; however, note that the aliases are strongly typed. You can only use User_Alias in a user field, and so on.
- The runas_user field is optional. It defaults to *root*, if not present.
- If you specify a path to an executable with nothing after it, an authorized user can add any argument they like to it. Contrariwise, if you specify arguments, they can only use the arguments you specify.
- Paths to executables should be full paths. The user can use $PATH normally to use the shortened form, but you should give the long form in the sudoers file.

The full syntax for sudo is even more complex. There are many more options and tweaks that can be used. To find out more about them, see the sudoers file's manpage or visit http://www.sudo.ws.

Direct root use now blocked by default

Previously, at manual system installation time, the OS installer would prompt you for a root password. Now, in addition to that, it will prompt you for the name/password of a user account intended to be the day-to-day account of the sysadmin.

If you follow along with this path, you will find out to your chagrin that you can no longer log in as root!

Attempts to log in as user *root* will be met with the complaint "Roles cannot log in directly". Instead, to run commands as root, you will be expected to use either `sudo` (with your own password) or `su` (with the root password).

If you find yourself in this situation and it does not sit well with you, don't panic! You can restore root to its full account status by editing the file `/etc/user_attr` and setting root's entry to be `type=normal` rather than `type=role`.

Fine-grained RBAC privileges

While **Role-Based Access Control (RBAC)** has been a part of Solaris for a long time now, Solaris 11 provides a few new knobs to play with. It is now possible to fine tune a user or process's ability to read or write a file, independently of each other. It is also possible to grant or take away the ability to have network access.

The specific new privileges are named, not surprisingly, `file_read`, `file_write`, and `net_access`.

It should be noted that `net_access` also affects the ability to use InterProcess Communication (IPC) mechanisms.

To take away a particular user's ability in one of these areas, use the `usermod` command as follows:

```
usermod -K defaultpriv=basic,!file_write targetuser
```

On-disk encryption

ZFS in Solaris 11 now also offers optional on-disk encryption. Some additional coverage of this is given in *Chapter 6, ZFS – Now You Can't Ignore It!*. The Solaris Cryptographic Framework libraries are used for encryption purposes, so ZFS will receive the benefit of any compatible crypto acceleration present on the system.

As an additional point of interest, the *inherited* nature of encrypted filesystems means that if a global zone creates a /zones filesystem, and then creates a zone with a zoneroots underneath, the zone will have the benefit of on-disk encryption without ever having direct access to the encryption key itself.

Warnings about encrypted ZFS filesystems

There are some gotchas to using a encrypted ZFS filesystem that should be carefully considered before using:

- Once you enable encryption on a ZFS filesystem, it cannot be turned off.

- Encryption will also be enabled on all subfilesystems, irrevocably.

- You cannot use zfs send/zfs receive for a non-encrypted ZFS destination.

- If you choose to enable ZFS filesystem encryption, there may be some degree of performance penalty: either from slightly increased CPU burden on the system or a minute delay in writes.

- While it is possible to change the encryption key for a filesystem, the new key will only apply to newly written data. Preexisting data on the filesystem will remain encrypted with the prior key(s).

- Encryption requires keys, which require key management; this is mentioned in the next section.

Creating an encrypted ZFS filesystem

To create an encrypted ZFS filesystem is deceptively easy. For a trivial case, you can enable encryption with a manually typed passphrase:

```
zfs create -o encryption=on zpool/encrypted
```

You will then be prompted for a passphrase, similar to when you create a GPG key or PKCS-type key/certificate.

As with those, the passphrase is not the actual encryption key but serves to authorize access to the private encryption key, which is automatically generated and embedded within the filesystem itself.

If you do nothing else, every time you need to mount the filesystem (which will presumably be included every time you need to reboot the system) ZFS will prompt for someone to input the passphrase.

Alternatively, you can have the passphrase stored in a file, a PKCS11 container, or to a particular HTTPS URL.

A file location for a passphrase can be extended in its flexibility by referencing removable media as a location. While at first glance specifying an HTTPS URL sounds unsecure, it is better than it sounds; since, with properly handled HTTPS, a network sniffer can only see what port you connect to and not the actual URL. Thus, `https://my.server/keys/random_filename_here` is fairly secure as long as the `keys` directory is not publicly readable.

To change the location or type of key handling, you may adjust the `keysource` property for the filesystem. Two examples of this would be as follows:

```
zfs set keysource=passphrase,prompt

zfs set,\
keysource=hex,https://secure.server/keys/bonnie_blue_bells.txt
```

Interaction between encryption, compression, and deduplication

ZFS encryption is designed to play well with the complimentary features of compression and deduplication. When data is written to a filesystem with all three features enabled, the data is first compressed and then encrypted. Finally, deduplication is applied when appropriate.

PKCS11 centralized key store support

Solaris 10 has supported local certificate and key management, including management of PKCS11 objects via `pktool`. PKCS11 support has been further augmented in Solaris 11. As mentioned previously, an option for ZFS encryption is to use PKCS11 keys. In a sense, this configuration can make a Solaris 11 installation a data encryption device similar to a tape library that supports automatic encryption.

With this in mind, Oracle now supports integration with its **Oracle Key Manager** product. This is a product designed for large scale, centralized PKCS11 key management, with a comprehensive GUI and access controls. While originally marketed as a tool for hardware-based storage devices, a Solaris 11 server's needs will be accommodated by it just as well.

Profiles can now be in LDAP

Profiles have been around in Solaris for quite some years now, as a method of granting access to things that are far more powerful than Unix groups. They allow for individual RBAC permissions to be granted and revoked in a batch-like manner. Their big limitation was that they were only able to be configured on a local-system basis.

In Solaris 11, this limitation has been lifted by allowing LDAP as a configuration backend.

Additional encryption support

Additional allowed algorithms have been added to Solaris's IPSEC/IKE framework. There has also been more hardware support added to the built-in cryptographic libraries, such as SPARC T4 onboard encryption and Intel CPU-based AES acceleration.

Summary

Solaris 11 is serious about security. Its default configuration is to be secure, and allows you to tighten down the box even further with its pre-enabled auditing and available on-disk encryption. The ability to have fully read-only zones is possibly the ultimate *secure server*, if you don't count resorting to an appliance running purely out of ROM. Oracle has taken its enterprise mentality and applied it to Solaris security with great effectiveness.

9
Miscellaneous

And then, there's this other stuff...

What's in this chapter anyway?

Every general-purpose book has a miscellaneous chapter. This is it for ours! Perhaps you might think that some of the things here belong in a different chapter. However, as Michelangelo is purported to have said:

> *"Perfection is achieved not when there is nothing more to add, but when there is nothing left to take away."*

Under his tutelage, I took it away from that chapter, and put it here instead!

Sadly, that may make this chapter less than perfect, but I hope you find some of the things here of interest anyway. The top three and most eye-catching ones in this chapter are:

- The return of text-based virtual consoles
- SMF transition automated alerts
- iSCSI management changes

Virtual consoles, also known as virtual terminals, are back

A few revisions ago, Solaris x86 had the popular **virtual consoles** code (popular with many other free OSs) shoehorned in. I, for one, was saddened when they took it out, supposedly for being inconsistent with the overall Solaris kernel tree. Happily, they have decided to bring it back. (Although not for SPARC. Boo!) Note that they are properly referred to now as **virtual terminals (VTs)**.

If you are not familiar with the virtual consoles concept, it allows you to have multiple text-based consoles without running a window system. Picture a text-based console. Then imagine you have a few extras hidden away that you can switch between with a keyboard sequence. The sequence in question is a three-key combo, as follows:

Ctrl + Alt + (F1 through F7)

F1 switches to VT #1. *F2* switches to VT #2, and so on. By default, and by convention, when you start up an X window session, it uses VT #7. Likewise, the "normal" (or original, boot-time) console is VT #1.

This can be very useful if you want to have multiple local sessions while being ultra-miserly on RAM or if you've managed to hang the X server on a minimally networked machine.

It is important to note that the method for enabling VTs is completely different from before, and it is not enabled by default.

There is a special daemon that takes care of interpreting the hotkeys on a console and switching between the VTs. If it is not already running, you may enable it with the following steps:

```
svcadm enable vtdaemon
svcadm enable console-login:vt2   //and so on, up to vt6, if you wish
```

Fast reboot

Solaris 11 is capable of doing a **fast reboot**, skipping the power-on style self tests that have traditionally accompanied a reboot.

On x86 machines, this will automatically happen if you use the `reboot` command. To force a full test cycle, and/or to get access to the **boot order** menu from the BIOS, use `halt`, followed by pressing a key.

On SPARC, the default configuration requires that you use `reboot -f` for a fast reboot. If you wish fast reboot to be the default on SPARC, you must override an SMF property, as follows:

```
# svccfg -s "system/boot-config:default" setprop\
config/fastreboot_default=true
```

```
# svcadm refresh svc:/system/boot-config:default
```

To temporarily override the setting and reboot the slow way, you can use `reboot -p`, aka "reboot to PROM".

CUPS printing

The CUPS printing system is now the standard backend printing mechanism on Solaris 11. Some old backend tools are not just deprecated but ripped out. Things such as `/usr/lib/lp/bin/netpr` are no longer available although certain printing *filters* still are. The good news is that things such as `/bin/lp` still look more or less the same to the user, and if you really need it, you can still enable assorted protocol bridge services to CUPS for things such as rfc1179, IPP, or PAPI.

Describing the CUPS printing system in full would not be a good use of space in this book. Oracle has a 300-page admin document entirely dedicated to CUPS printing (document ID *821-1457*).

Instead, you might try reading the full documentation at `http://cups.org`, or you could just make your life easy by running the `system-config-printer` GUI tool, either from `xterm` or by pulling down the Oracle GNOME menus and navigating to **System – Administration – Print Manager**.

Power management

The old `pmconfig` command has been replaced by the following tool, which fits in with the new naming standards nicely:

```
poweradm
```

As might be expected, this tool stores most of its configurations in the SMF database rather than in `/etc/power.conf`.

To see a list of values, you can use the following command:

```
# poweradm list
active_control/administrative-authority    smf=platform,
current=platform
suspend/suspend-enable                      smf=false, current=false
active_config/time-to-full-capacity         platform=250, current=250
active_config/time-to-minimum-responsiveness  platform=0, current=0
disabled                                     platform=false
```

Paraphrasing a little, the preceding output shows that "the system does not have power management disabled". It also shows that "the system does not have suspend/resume capabilities", if it has not been changed. By default, if the machine hardware is capable of suspend/resume, the value will be set to true.

The other values can be accessed by their right-most component rather than by the full name. For example, you can display just the suspend-enable capability by:

```
# poweradm get suspend-enable
```

The time-to-full-capacity and time-to-minimum-responsiveness values are restraints for the system's power management. Only power conservation methods that can stay within the specified constraints will be employed.

The values for these two settings can be taken from the SMF database or directly from the "platform" (that is, BIOS or Service Processor). The default is to take them from platform settings. To override them with SMF values, use the following command:

```
# poweradm set administrative-authority=smf
```

Be warned, however, that executing the preceding command may cause the system to go directly into maintenance mode, depending on what values are set for time-to-full-capacity and time-to-minimum-responsiveness.

To get the system quickly back into fully functional mode, you can perform the following steps:

```
# poweradm set administrative-authority=none
# poweradm set time-to-full-capacity=somevalue
# poweradm set time-to-minimum-responsiveness=somevalue
# svcadm clear power
```

Notifications triggered by SMF state transitions

SMF has learned a new trick with Solaris 11; it can now tell you when services alter state. This is done via the new `svccfg` subcommand, `setnotify`.

It is possible to send notifications via SNMP or e-mail. It is also possible to set up notifications for individual services or for all services at once.

SMF notifications through e-mail, also known as SMTP

Compare the following two examples for setting up e-mail alerts:

```
// To email when any service goes into or comes out of maintenance state:
svccfg setnotify -g maintenance mailto:root@mycompany.com


// To email when just this service transitions
svccfg -s mysvcname setnotify maintenance mailto:root@mycompany.com
```

 -g does not mean "goes to". It is a flag for "global". Do not mix it with a line intended for an individual service, or you will get many more notifications than you have planned!

There are many other transition types and state names. It is possible to alert only transitions to a state, or transitions out of a state, by state tags such as `from-maintenance` and `to-maintenance`. You may also wish to reference the `smtp-notify` package's manpage.

SMF notifications through SNMP

At this time, SMF does not have its own direct SNMP configuration. It shares the Oracle SNMP configuration file. As such, if you wish to use SNMP alerts for SMF, you may first need to install the `snmp-notify` package. Next, you will need to configure a `trapsync` line in `/etc/net-snmp/snmp/snmpd.conf` to configure where SNMP alerts are sent. Finally, you will need to configure a service to use SNMP. As with e-mail notifications, you can do this for individual services or all services.

```
// pkg install snmp-notify, if you don't have it already.
// Next, add a trapsync line, and refresh your snmp daemon, if you do
// not have one configured
echo 'trapsync your.snmp.watcher community-string-here'
>>/etc/net-snmp/snmp/snmpd.conf
svcadm refresh net-snmp:default


// To send an SNMP trap when any service goes into or comes out of
// maintenance state:
svccfg setnotify -g maintenance snmp:


// To send an SNMP trap when just this service transitions
svccfg -s mysvcname setnotify maintenance snmp:


// Please note that the trailing ":" after "snmp", is crucial!
```

If you forget, this is referenced in the *svccfg* manpage, under the *setnotify* section. There is also a separate manpage for `snmp-notify`.

Querying and deleting SMF notifications

To see what type of notifications (if any) have been set, use `svccfg listnotify`.

To clear particular configured notifications, use the `delnotify` subcommand with the same syntax used for `setnotify`.

Trusted Solaris extras

Solaris Trusted Extensions (what used to be known as "Trusted Solaris") isn't dead yet! Oracle is still improving and refining Solaris integration with Trusted Extensions for those spooky folks who require things such as mandatory security access levels for all data. I can't tell you what all the changes are (or I'd have to kill you!), but suffice it to say that the `txzonemgr` GUI tool (now available via GNOME libraries only) has had some updating for RBAC and the like, to the point where it can now be used to *manage* most aspects of Trusted Extensions.

COMSTAR and iSCSI

Following its general unification mantra, Oracle has decided to also attempt to unify SCSI device configuration under a new shared umbrella called the **COmmon Multiprotocol SCSI TARget (COMSTAR)** framework.

That's the good news. The bad news is that Oracle has departed from its hitherto intuitive naming by not fully leveraging the sensibly named `iscsiadm` command. Previously, that command was purposed to handle iSCSI initiators rather than all iSCSI duties. Rather than extending its duties, however, Oracle has decided to perform a sidegrade via the SCSI Target Mode Framework (`stmfadm`) command. The new command is meant to be a general interface for SCSI target operations, such as security for allowing access to data. That said, for iSCSI-specific target side duties, the `iscsiadm` command is still the way to go.

For handling the iSCSI target side of things, there is now `itadm`. It is exclusively for **iSCSI targets**. Try not to confuse the initial "i" for "initiator". It's the exact opposite!

Targets are references to a data volume or set of data volumes (aka LUNs). In contrast, initiators identify systems attempting to read/write a target. They are somewhat equivalent to the concept of **SCSI Host Bus Adaptors (HBAs)**.

Also in the good news/bad news category is that sharing a ZFS volume as an iSCSI target is no longer done by simply setting a `shareiscsi` property in ZFS. Now, any device can potentially be shared, so a ZFS volume device is treated just like any other device. So, while it doesn't show up quite as clearly in ZFS any more, there is at least a certain amount of consistency to it.

iSCSI targets

Here is an example of setting up a ZFS volume as an iSCSI target, with basic security based on initiator filters:

```
// If you haven't already, install the required packages, and enable the
// appropriate services:
pkg install iscsi-target scsi-target-mode-framework

svcadm enable -r iscsi/target

// The "-r" is CRITICAL!
```

```
// Next, create an iSCSI reference for your host, aka an IQN label.
// You can either use the default, or specify a more meaningful name
// This is highly recommended, since default looks like
//   iqn.1986-03.com.sun:02:1d5dcfbf-a19c-6c95-a470-f239c786be7d
itadm create-target -n iqn.2010.com.your.host:myprettylabel


// Next, create a container of trusted initiators, called a "host group"
stmfadm create-hg secure-group
stmfadm add-hg-member -g secure-group iqn.2010.com.your.host


// Create a volume to serve as your data source
zfs create -V 10g datapool/somevol


// Finally, associate the ZFS volume with an internal LU/LUN ID,
// and then make that ID accessible to the host initiators
// specified in the host group created above
stmfadm create-lu /dev/zvol/rdsk/datapool/somevol
stmfadm list-lu
stmfadm add-view -h secure-group {LONG-LU-FROM-list-lu}


// If you forget in future which host groups have access,
// use list-lu:
stmfadm list-view -l {LONG-LU-FROM-list-lu}
```

It is also possible to set up CHAP authentication on a per-target basis and even to integrate with a RADIUS server. For details, see the *itadm(1M)* manpage or the full Oracle COMSTAR documentation at http://docs.oracle.com.

iSCSI initiator mode

To enable a Solaris 11 host to access iSCSI targets elsewhere, you must first configure an initiator and then point it at any devices you wish the host to access:

```
// First add the package, if you do not have it already.
// Then enable the prerequisite service
pkg install iscsi-initiator
svcadm enable iscsi/initiator


// Next, tell your host what the IQN of the data is, and on what host
// it lives on.
//The simplest way is static configuration.
iscsiadm add static-config iqn.long.ugly.string.here IP.OF.SVR.HERE
iscsiadm modify discovery --static enable


// Alternatively, if you dont know the IQN, you might try autodiscovery
iscsiadm add discovery-address IP.OF.SVR.HERE
iscsiadm modify discovery --sendtargets enable


// Finally, give the disk driver layer a nudge to rescan devices
devfsadm -C -i iscsi
```

Once the last `devfsadm` command is done, the new iSCSI device should show up in format, ready for you to use.

Removing remote iSCSI devices

While adding extra storage to a host via remote iSCSI targets is relatively easy (presuming you have a good, fast network), it can sometimes lead to frustrating problems at startup if a device is not available or even if one LUN has previously been recognized. For this reason, it is sometimes wisest to stick to static configuration mode since it is the easiest and fastest to clean up. However, the method of removal of both types of iSCSI device is given here.

It is best, whenever possible, to follow good sysadmin practices of cleanly unmounting the relevant devices before removing their configuration details via the following step!

```
// If you used static-config above, then just remove the same entry
iscsiadm remove static-config iqn.long.ugly.string.here IP.OF.SVR.HERE
//If on the other hand, you used autodiscovery, you may have to
 disable ALL devices on a target host, by removing the host address:
iscsiadm remove discovery-address IP.OF.SVR.HERE


// When the system is extremely unhappy, you may wish to turn off all
// forms of discovery one by one. First static, then the
// autodiscovery method is shown here
iscsiadm modify discovery -static disable
iscsiadm modify discovery -sendtarget disable


// You may also attempt to remove individual iqn referenced targets.
itadm delete-target iqn.long.ugly.string.here
// In very extreme cases, itadm offers a -f(orce) option. There is
// also an "offline-target" option to stmfadm
```

There is a third kind of iSCSI target referencing, called iSNS. If you require details on that, please see the Oracle iSCSI documentation.

Safeguarding complex iSCSI configurations

It should be mentioned that, if a complex iSCSI related configuration has been created, it can be backed up or restored through the SMF svccfg utility, for example, as in the following commands:

```
svccfg export -a stmf  >stmf.export.cfg
svccfg import stmf.export.cfg
```

Summary

It's unfortunate that there doesn't seem to be a good category to group these items in, but you never know when they may come in handy. Give the chapter a quick rescan, and your brain may be tickled a few months from now that there is a solution to your curious problem du jour after all.

A
IPS Package Reference

Some information tables have been moved out of the related chapters because sometimes it's nice to have all the "quick reference" tables in the same place. So, these useful tables are covered in this appendix as well as in *Appendix B, New ACL Permissions and Abbreviations*, and *Appendix C, Solaris 10 Available Enhancements*. Additionally, the Solaris 10 information does not officially fit into a "What's new in Solaris 11?" format book. But the information is useful to Solaris 10 sysadmins considering a transition to Solaris 11.

Not all the IPS commands are listed in the following table, but you will find most of the day-to-day commands that you'll need:

IPS command	Solaris 10 equivalent	Purpose
pkg info -l {names}	pkginfo -l {names}	Detailed information on packages
pkg install {name}	pkgadd -d somefile.pkg	Install a package
pkg list {names}	pkginfo {names}	List packages installed
pkg list -a {name}	N/a	Show installed and available packages (usually with some kind of target search string)
pkg list -u	N/a	List packages with available updates
pkg update -nv	N/a	Show impact of available updates
pkg update {name)	patchadd ######-##	Patch a package
pkg search /some/path	grep /some/path /var/sadm/install/contents	Find what package contains a file. Use shell-style wildcards with pkg search.
pkg search basename:file	grep '/file ' /var/sadm/install/contents	Find what package contains a file, without the full path
pkg contents pkg/name	grep 'SUNWxyz' /var/sadm/install/contents	Find what files are in a package

B

New ACL Permissions and Abbreviations

As mentioned in *Chapter 6, ZFS – Now You Can't Ignore It*, chmod is now responsible for setting ACLs on files. It allows for both a long form and a short form. For convenience, here is a simple table of all ACL types. Please note that some things are only applicable to files, or conversely, to directories. Additionally, sometimes you must use a different verbose name for directories versus files.

It is nice to note that the old standby rwx letter abbreviations in chmod mean the same thing they always have. For convenience, here again is the example usage given previously, to allow user mysql to write to the file /etc/zshrc. The first line is equivalent in result to the second one:

```
chmod A+user:mysql:write_data:allow/etc/zshrc
chmod A+user:mysql:w:allow/etc/zshrc
```

The following is a table with the full set of allowable ACLs:

Abbreviation	Verbose parameter
a	read_attributes
A	write_attributes
c	read_acl (allowed to see what the ACLs are)
C	write_acl (allowed to set ACLs)
d	delete (the file)
D (directory only)	delete_child
O	write_owner (change owner of file/directory)
p (file only)	append_data (not implemented yet)
p (directory only)	add_subdirectory

Abbreviation	Verbose parameter
r (file only)	read_data
r (directory only)	list_directory
S	synchronize (not implemented yet)
R	read_xattr (extended attributes)
w	write_data
W	write_xattr (extended attributes)
x	execute

C
Solaris 10 Available Enhancements

Some highly useful features were introduced for Solaris 11 but were also backported to Solaris 10 as part of **Maintenance Update 10 (MU10)**, or in some cases, earlier updates.

ZFS backported enhancements

The primary points of interest are related to ZFS. They are already mentioned in *Chapter 6, ZFS – Now You Can't Ignore It*, as being potentially available in Solaris 10, but they are significant enough that they are worth calling out in an explicitly named section here.

The big feature additions of automatic compression, deduplication, and `zfs diff` can all be added into Solaris 10 via patching. Please refer to the relevant chapter for full details on how to use them.

Additionally, a significant bug related to free space and speed was patched in ZFS. It used to be such that, once any ZFS filesystem reached 80 percent, a significant performance hit was taken by any writes occurring on that filesystem and potentially anywhere in the same pool.

To get the fix for this (as well as to enable the newer features) it is crucial to fully patch the Solaris 10 system *and also* to upgrade both the ZFS pool version and the ZFS filesystem version, wherever these things are a concern.

Please note that, while the ZFS pool version update is relatively fast and painless, the ZFS filesytem update is not. Running `zfs upgrade` can take minutes, if not hours, on a full filesystem and will write-lock the filesystem or, at best, heavily impact performance.

Other enhancements

Fast reboot for SPARC is also available in fully patched versions of Solaris 10. (Fast reboot is mentioned in *Chapter 9, Miscellaneous*.)

Index

Thank you for buying
Oracle Solaris 11: First Look

About Packt Publishing

Packt, pronounced 'packed', published its first book "Mastering phpMyAdmin for Effective MySQL Management" in April 2004 and subsequently continued to specialize in publishing highly focused books on specific technologies and solutions.

Our books and publications share the experiences of your fellow IT professionals in adapting and customizing today's systems, applications, and frameworks. Our solution based books give you the knowledge and power to customize the software and technologies you're using to get the job done. Packt books are more specific and less general than the IT books you have seen in the past. Our unique business model allows us to bring you more focused information, giving you more of what you need to know, and less of what you don't.

Packt is a modern, yet unique publishing company, which focuses on producing quality, cutting-edge books for communities of developers, administrators, and newbies alike. For more information, please visit our website: www.packtpub.com.

About Packt Enterprise

In 2010, Packt launched two new brands, Packt Enterprise and Packt Open Source, in order to continue its focus on specialization. This book is part of the Packt Enterprise brand, home to books published on enterprise software – software created by major vendors, including (but not limited to) IBM, Microsoft and Oracle, often for use in other corporations. Its titles will offer information relevant to a range of users of this software, including administrators, developers, architects, and end users.

Writing for Packt

We welcome all inquiries from people who are interested in authoring. Book proposals should be sent to author@packtpub.com. If your book idea is still at an early stage and you would like to discuss it first before writing a formal book proposal, contact us; one of our commissioning editors will get in touch with you.

We're not just looking for published authors; if you have strong technical skills but no writing experience, our experienced editors can help you develop a writing career, or simply get some additional reward for your expertise.

Oracle WebCenter 11g PS3 Administration Cookbook

ISBN: 978-1-84968-228-2   Paperback: 348 pages

Over 100 advanced recipes to secure, support, manage, and administer Oracle WebCenter

Oracle WebCenter 11g PS3
Administration Cookbook

Over 100 advanced Recipes to secure, support, manage, and administer Oracle WebCenter

Yannick Ongena

1. The only book and eBook in the market that focuses on administration tasks using the new features of WebCenter 11g PS3

2. Understand the use of Wiki and Discussion services to build collaborative portals

3. Full of illustrations, diagrams, and tips with clear step-by-step instructions and real-world examples

4. Learn how to build rich enterprise 2.0 portals with WebCenter 11g

Oracle Weblogic Server 11gR1 PS2: Administration Essentials

ISBN: 978-1-84968-302-9   Paperback: 304 pages

Install, configure, deploy, and administer Java EE applications with Oracle WebLogic Server

Oracle WebLogic Server 11gR1 PS2:
Administration Essentials

Install, configure, deploy, and administer Java EE applications with Oracle WebLogic Server

Michel Schildmeijer

1. A practical book with step-by-step instructions for admins in real-time company environments

2. Create, commit, undo, and monitor a change session using the Administration Console

3. Create basic automated tooling with WLST

4. Access advanced resource attributes in the Administration Console

Please check **www.PacktPub.com** for information on our titles

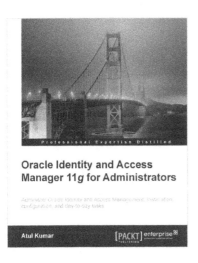

Oracle Identity and Access Manager 11g for Administrators

Oracle Identity and Access Manager 11g for Administrators

ISBN: 978-1-84968-268-8   Paperback: 336 pages

Administer Oracle Identity and Access Management: Installation, configuration, and day-to-day tasks

1. Full of illustrations, diagrams, and tips with clear step-by-step instructions and real time examples

2. Understand how to Integrate OIM/OAM with E-Business Suite, Webcenter, Oracle Internet Directory and Active Directory

3. Learn various techniques for implementing and managing OIM/OAM with illustrative screenshots

4. Configure Authentication/Authorization schemes, resources, host identifiers, and application domain in Oracle Access Manager

Oracle BPM Suite 11g Developer's cookbook

ISBN: 978-1-84968-422-4   Paperback: 512 pages

Over 80 advanced recipes to develop rich, interactive business processes using the oracle Business Process Management Suite

1. Full of illustrations, diagrams, and tips with clear step-by-step instructions and real time examples to develop Industry Sample BPM Process and BPM interaction with SOA Components

2. Dive into lessons on Fault ,Performance and Rum Time Management

3. Explore User Interaction ,Deployment and Monitoring

Please check **www.PacktPub.com** for information on our titles